Dreams and Visions Workshop

A RESOURCE FOR SMALL GROUP STUDY

Colette Toach

www.ami-bookshop.com

Dreams and Visions Workshop
A Resource for Small Group Study

ISBN-10: 1-62664-151-X
ISBN-13: 978-1-62664-151-8

Copyright © 2016 by Apostolic Movement International, LLC
All rights reserved
5663 Balboa Ave #416,
San Diego,
California 92111,
United States of America

1st Printing August 2016

Published by **Apostolic Movement International, LLC**
E-mail Address: admin@ami-bookshop.com
Web Address: www.ami-bookshop.com

All rights reserved under International Copyright Law.
Contents may not be reproduced in whole or in part in any form without the express written consent of the publisher.

Unless specified, all Scripture references taken from the New King James Version®. Copyright © 1982 by Thomas Nelson. Used by permission. All rights reserved.

Dedication

Who could have imagined in the year 2000, that a simple message I entitled "Dream Interpretation by the Spirit" would become a revolution into what I understood dream and vision interpretation to be.

It was not long before a message became a series, which became a book, which became a course in our Prophetic School…

Following on its heels, *The Way of Dreams and Visions Symbol Dictionary* made its first appearance in 2011, and now you hold in your hands the *Dreams and Visions Workshop – A Resource for Small Group Study*.

You never know all the things God has in store for you, until you take that first step. What started out as a step has become a movement – one I no longer walk on my own. To get this project into your hands, hours of travail, prayer, and work was invested into every inked word.

I might have received the inspiration, but I rode on the wings of my team who have invested tirelessly into this project. So, I do not take the credit, but want to dedicate this publication to my wondering spiritual family and A.M.I. Team members (You know who you are!). From each country, walk of life and calling, we all pulled together to make this happen.

Our goal is the same – to see you rise up into the fullness of your call! Our reward is the fruit that is birthed in your spiritual life through these teachings.

Contents

Dedication 3
Introduction – How to Use This Workshop 8
   The Materials 8
   How to Use This Book 9
   Study Methods 10
   Re-teach the Principles 14
Part 01 – Dream Interpretation by the Spirit 16
   Lesson 01 – Dream Interpretation by the Spirit 16
   Lesson 02 – Prophetic Dreams 25
   Lesson 03 – External Prophetic Dreams 37
   Lesson 04 - Five P's In Dream Interpretation 47
Part 02 – Visions: Your Secret Conversation with God 60
   Lesson 05 - Visions: Your Secret Conversation with God 60
   Lesson 06 - Three Spiritual Functions 69
   Lesson 07 – Spiritual Fruit 81
   Lesson 08 – Receiving Visions 93
Part 03 - Nightmares, Deception and Demonic Dreams 106
   Lesson 09 - Nightmares, Deception and Demonic Dreams 106
   Lesson 10 - The Signs of Deception 119
Part 04 - Interpreting Symbols in Dreams and Visions 134
   Lesson 11 – Interpreting Symbols in Dreams and Visions 134
   Lesson 12 - Interpreting Characters in Dreams and Visions 149
   Lesson 13 - Gender and Race in Dreams and Visions 159
   Lesson 14 - Examples of Gender and Race 167
Part 05 - Experiencing the Realm of the Spirit 180
   Lesson 15 - Experiencing the Realm of the Spirit 180
   Lesson 16 - Visions and Warfare 189
   Lesson 17 - Developing Your Relationship with God 197

Lesson 18 - Edification of the Body	207
Part 06 - Interpreting for Others	220
Lesson 19 - Interpreting for Others	220
Lesson 20 - Interpreting Internal Dreams	231
Part 07 - Spiritual Revelation and Discernment	242
Lesson 21 - Revelation and Discernment	242
Lesson 22 - Four Pointers for Interpretation	251
Exercise Answers	266
Lesson 01	266
Lesson 02	267
Lesson 03	268
Lesson 04	270
Lesson 08	271
Lesson 15	272
Lesson 20	273
Lesson 21	274
Lesson 22	275
Where to From Here	284
About the Author	286
Contact Information	287

INTRODUCTION

HOW TO USE THIS BOOK

INTRODUCTION – HOW TO USE THIS WORKSHOP

JUST ADD PASSION

You hold in your hands, everything you need to interpret dreams and visions. From symbol interpretation, hearing the voice of God for yourself, and knowing how to tap into the spirit – you have it all.

All that you need to add, is passion! Apostle Paul tells us to earnestly desire the gifts. You can have all the resources in the world, but without the passion to draw closer to God, they are empty words on a blank page.

So before you begin the first lesson, approach this book with hunger! Hunger to hear from the Lord. Hunger to go deeper into the realm of the Holy Spirit, and hunger to teach God's people what God has shown you.

THE MATERIALS

This workshop is based on the following resources:

1. The Way of Dreams and Visions Book
2. The Dreams and Visions Symbol Dictionary
3. The Dreams and Visions Workshop (In hand)
4. The Way of Dreams and Visions Audio MP3 CD (in hand)

DO I NEED ALL FOUR RESOURCES?

I suggest getting all four if you are going to take full advantage of this workshop. However, you can get away with the bare minimum of *The Way of Dreams and Visions* book and the *Dreams and Visions Workshop*.

Every lesson in this workshop is based directly on the teachings of the *Way of Dreams and Visions* book.

KEY POINTS TO KEEP IN MIND

1. Every lesson in this workshop is based on a chapter in *The Way of Dreams and Visions* book.

2. *The Way of Dreams and Visions Audio MP3 CD* contains the audio teachings of the book. Please note though, that the book will contain more elements and a format that is laid out in more detail. I suggest having both in hand for effective study.
3. Answers for exercises are at the end of the workshop.

How to Use This Book

7 PARTS. 22 LESSONS

This workbook is split up into 7 parts. Each of these parts is based on each of the audio MP3 messages. In *The Way of Dreams and Visions* book, these messages have been broken down further into 23 chapters in total.

From these 23 chapters, I have complied 22 lessons in this workshop, for you to study.

As you read through this book, you will see different sections in each lesson:

1. Notes
2. Questions for Review
3. Practical Project
4. Exercise
5. Group Project

NOTES

Every lesson contains additional notes to drive the points home that you already learned in *The Way of Dreams and Visions* book or audio MP3 CD.

You are welcome to skip these notes if you do not like to read. They will add to your knowledge, but if you do not read them, you will still be able to complete the *Questions for Review* and the *Practical Projects*.

QUESTIONS FOR REVIEW

Each question is designed to help you retain knowledge. You will notice that this workshop is a blend of teaching you both knowledge, and wisdom. This section assists in helping you remember what you learned, so that the Holy Spirit has something to work with later on!

PRACTICAL PROJECT

If you do not live the knowledge you retained, it becomes dead manna in your spirit. To bring the principles to life, this section will make sure that they become your own! By applying the practical project, you will take what you have learned and turn it into a personal conviction.

It is not good enough to continue quoting what I teach! The principles must become your own. This is the core purpose of the practical projects, because when you live a principle, you will never forget it!

EXERCISE

This section will be a tremendous source of encouragement for you! It puts what you have learned and lived to the test. Here you will get to test out your interpretation abilities and see if you have retained everything you learned. Because it is neatly written out in this workshop, is is also a risk-free way of learning. You never need to worry about getting an answer wrong.

There is no such thing as "wrong answers" for an exercise – only learning opportunities! If your answer does not line up with the provided solution, then your learning goes up a level. You will come to realize that you learn more when you get the answers wrong, than if you always get them right. So cut yourself some slack and enjoy this journey!

GROUP PROJECT

At the end of each part, you will see a project intended for group study. Each project is based on each of the audio MP3 messages. I will give you instruction on how to conduct a *Group Study* further down.

STUDY METHODS

You will see that I have designed this workshop with a variety of options.

1. Self Study
2. Group Study
3. Re-teach the Principles

SELF STUDY

Taking the materials, you have everything you need to become an expert on dream and vision interpretation.

Because you are holding the Dreams and Visions Workshop in your hand, you are ready to get moving!

1. Pop in the MP3 CD and begin by listening to the *Dream Interpretation by the Spirit*.
2. Then pick up the *Way of Dreams and Visions* book and read through chapter 1.
3. Start Lesson 1 by reading through the notes and make your way to your first *Questions for Review*
4. Work through the *Practical Projects* and the *Exercise*
5. Mark your answers! You will find the answers for all questions at the back of the Workshop

GROUP STUDY

Establishing a group study in a church or Christian study group is the core purpose of this workshop! Not only does it make studying a lot more interesting, but you will learn more as you help one another out in the interpretation purpose.

I promise, you will never have a dull meeting!

At our ministry centers, it is quite common to have a dream interpretation session! We do not plan it, but that is usually the time when everyone talks about the dreams they had the night before. Because we all know the principles outlined in these teachings, I will say this... breakfast is never boring!

Often it leads to ministry or a good laugh as our dreams confirm what God has been trying to say all week!

With that being said, you have two options for your group study. You can opt to have:

1. A 22 Week Study Group
2. A 7 Week Study Group

THE 22 WEEK STUDY GROUP

If you have the time and want to do a comprehensive study, then you can complete one lesson a week with your group.

This is perfect if you are doing other courses at the same time and cannot overwhelm your group with too much information at one given time.

HOW TO PROCEED

1. Begin your first session by reading through Chapter 1 of *The Way of Dreams and Visions* book
2. Open up your workbook and have someone else read the *Notes*
3. From there proceed to the *Questions for Review*

You have the option of getting everyone to fill in the answers on their own in the group, or you can opt to answer them out loud together.

4. Read over the *Practical Project* and inform the group that it is their responsibility to complete this at home, before coming to the next meeting.
5. Complete your session by doing the *Exercise* together

HOMEWORK

At the end of each session, remind everyone to complete their practical project that week and to listen to the next audio MP3 message.

Because there are only 7 MP3 messages, everyone only needs to listen to that message when beginning each part. Every part is clearly laid out in the workbook and the title of the MP3 is clearly written out.

REACHING THE END OF THE FIRST PART

At the end of Lesson 4, you will see that there is a group study for you to participate in. You can opt to do the *Exercise* and the *Group Project* for this meeting, or you can skip the exercise and just do the *Group Project*.

TESTING AND CERTIFICATION

If you would like to provide certification at the end of this study, you are welcome to select questions from each of the *Questions for Review* and compile your own "test" at the end of the workshop. You can then provide certificates of completion with your own ministry letterhead.

CONGRATULATIONS! YOU ARE FINISHED!

Because you chose the 22-week option, a celebration at the end is highly recommended! Your group has worked hard and been diligent. You do not realize how much you have all changed. End your final class with a celebration that includes your church or ministry.

THE 7 WEEK STUDY GROUP

This is the more popular method of study and enables you to complete the entire teaching in less than two months. It is long enough for the principles to sink in, but short enough that most people can find the time to attend the study group.

Instead of completing all 22 lessons with your group, you are going to work through one part at a time (7 parts in total). This allows you to be very flexible in what you want to teach and emphasize according to your group.

Now, this is going to require you to do a bit of work before each session. Before you start a session, you will need to do the following:

1. Work through all the *Questions for Review* of Part 1 and select the questions that you want the group to answer. Mark them in your own book.
2. Work through all the *Practical Projects* in Part 1 and select the project that is most suited to your group. You might also decide to give different attendees different projects according to their needs
3. Do the same with the *Exercise* – Select the ones you want to emphasize.

This enables you to tweak each study group according to the maturity and needs of the people attending.

HOW TO PROCEED

So how will a meeting look? Let me break it down for you and give you the Step 1, 2, 3…

Option 1: You can opt to read the first 5 chapters of the book together.

Option 2: Listen to the audio MP3 message, *Dream Interpretation by the Spirit*.

Option 3: If your time is short, then instruct everyone to do their required reading or to listen to the message on their own, before you meet.

1. Work through the required materials in *The Way of Dreams and Visions* book or audio MP3 CD
2. Answer the selected *Questions for Review* together. You can answer them quietly, or throw the questions around in discussion
3. Inform everyone on the practical project they need to concentrate on for that week.
4. Work through the exercise that you have picked out to see how everyone is coping with applying the principles
5. End with doing the *Group Project* supplied at the end of each part.

HOMEWORK

Everyone must leave with an understanding of which *Practical Project* to do the following week, along with any reading/listening they must do. (If you are not listening to the audio MP3 messages in your study)

RE-TEACH THE PRINCIPLES

You might feel that you want to take these principles on for yourself and teach them in your church or ministry. No problem! I have laid everything out as clearly as I could in all of my resources. All you need to do is pick through the ones that stood out the most for you.

PREPARE SERMON NOTES

Pick up *The Way of Dreams and Visions* book and use it to put together sermon notes.

1. You will notice that the book is divided into 23 chapters, but essentially 7 different parts. (These parts are based on the audio messages)
2. The book is divided into clear headings – larger ones for the main points and smaller ones for sub points.
3. Simply work through the book and pick out the headings that convey the main points you want to teach on.
4. From there select the sub headings.
5. Flesh your notes out.

PREPARE A PRACTICAL PROJECT

The Dreams and Visions Workshop gives you everything you need to put a project together that will allow everyone to live what you just taught!

Pick out the *Questions for Review, Practical Project* and *Exercise* that you feel would best suit your message. Compile these into a document and instruct everyone on how to complete them.

PART 01

DREAM INTERPRETATION BY THE SPIRIT

Part 01 – Dream Interpretation by the Spirit

> **KEY PRINCIPLE**
>
> The Lord will give you dreams that will answer the cry of your heart in the present. What are you praying for right now? What were you asking the Lord before bed? Your dream will likely be an answer to that.

Lesson 01 – Dream Interpretation by the Spirit

Based on: *The Way of Dreams and Visions*, Chapter 1

It's not about having the right teachings or knowledge when it comes to ministry. It is about living and experiencing the principles for yourself. So as you start getting into the teachings in this book, expect the Holy Spirit to come upon you with His anointing, so that you start living everything you are learning.

You see, this is not just about knowing, this is about being trained and experiencing ministry!

HELPING THE GARBAGE DREAMS TO COME TO AN END

When someone first starts to seek the Lord and get into the Word, those garbage dreams can get crazy. It might feel like all you are doing is throwing out junk. Now is not the time to get discouraged!

What I am going to show you here, is how to move on from there and also how to help someone break through in the Spirit as well.

The best thing that you can do, if you are having a ton of garbage dreams, is to press on! Continue to get into the Word, continue to get into the teaching, and continue to speak in tongues.

As you do this, after a while your spirit will start to clear, and the messages in your dreams will also start to clear up.

For many believers, the majority of their dream types are purging and garbage. Every now and again, an internal dream breaks through with a clear message from the Lord. The Lord desires more for them than that!

In the Old Testament, only the prophets and a select few heard from God in this way. In the New Testament, this ability is available to every believer! (Acts 2:17)

This means, that you should be encouraging believers to hear from the Lord in their dreams. Not only that, but teach them how to identify when God is speaking.

If they push through the garbage dreams and continue to get into the Word, then they will start experiencing more internal dreams.

WHEN YOUR PROPHETIC DREAMS DRY UP

Let us bring this home to your own ministry right now. If you have flowed well in prophetic dreams, but find that suddenly it came to a halt, now is not the time to panic! Like I said before, dreams are one of the first ways that God uses to speak to us.

As you mature in your walk with God, you will find that the Lord will start to use other means to speak to you. He will draw you into an intimate relationship with Him and you will start to hear from Him through visions, journaling and a face to face relationship.

In fact, as you start to interpret for others, you are going to be stretched! The Lord will not restrict His voice to your dreams any longer.

So if your prophetic dreams have "dried up" so to speak, do not panic! This does not mean that you have missed God! Instead, it means that you have started to mature and go to a new level in your walk with the Lord.

If your prophetic dreams dry up, it is a good sign indeed! The Lord is opening up a new opportunity for you.

NEW SYMBOLS IN YOUR DREAMS

Have you noticed, that as you get into new teaching or face new experiences, that you start noticing new symbols in your dreams? This is a good sign as well and it is an indication that you are receiving what God is showing you right now.

You will realize more and more in ministering to others, the symbols in their dreams reflect a part of themselves. So if you face a new circumstance in your life or perhaps a new crisis, a person from that situation might suddenly crop up in your dream.

What does this mean? It is very likely that from now on, that person is a representation of that era or failure in your life. So expect the symbols in your dreams to change and to adapt as you grow in the Lord.

As you minister to others, you might even find that you become a star in their dreams! If you have had a positive effect on the person's life, then it is likely that you represent the Holy Spirit in their dreams.

That is truly what makes dream interpretation so exciting! Just when you think you have it all figured out, something will happen that will turn the apple cart upside down. There is certainly no time to be bored!

As you go through this book, you might find that some of the symbols that I use here will crop up in your dreams. As your knowledge increases, the Holy Spirit is going to use that knowledge to speak to you. He will take the known, and then teach you the unknown.

It is the same for others that receive your ministry. The pictures and symbols you teach them, will suddenly crop up in their dreams. This is a good sign and it means that what you are sharing with them is making an impact on their lives!

God speaks through prophetic dreams and when you know how to interpret these dreams correctly, they are a powerful tool. However, I get very nervous with people that use their dreams as the "beginning and the end." They use it as the complete revelation that God has given to them.

DREAMS ARE A DOORWAY

I believe that God speaks in our dreams and that they are an open door of invitation into a greater realm. Interpreting dreams is like coming to a door with a key in your hand. When you can interpret that dream, it is like putting that key into the lock and opening the door.

However, once you are through the door, there is a greater way to touch the Lord. Dreams are but a doorway to developing a full relationship with the Lord. They are not the full experience.

The power is not the dream itself. The power lies in the application of the dream. Receiving a dream from the Lord, is only a step forward. It is when you apply the interpretation of that dream that you experience the power of it.

So when you interpret a dream correctly, it opens up the opportunity for you to teach others to hear from God in so many ways.

QUESTIONS FOR REVIEW

1. Who all is capable of receiving revelation through dreams and visions?

2. What dream type do only Christians have?

3. What 3 categories of dreams does all of mankind have?

4. How can you identify a healing dream?

5. How can you identify a cleansing/purging dream?

_____

_____

_____

_____

PRACTICAL PROJECT: STIRRING UP THE GIFTS

Before you can begin delving into dream and vision interpretation, it is vital that you stir up the spirit within and get rid of all the "junk" that has accumulated. For years, you have pushed down external pressures and influences of the world. All of these pressures and influences have colored your judgment and spiritual senses. So before you can hear clearly from the Lord, it is vital you clear that away.

How will you do that? By getting into the Word and the Spirit. By encouraging the gifts of revelation to be stirred within you, you will learn how to discern the anointing and also how to release it. Often you do not flow in the anointing, simply because you have not taken the time to feed on the Word, or you have not encouraged the Holy Spirit to pour out of you.

You have a spring of living water right inside of you! This project is going to tap into that spring and allow the Holy Spirit to begin leading and training you Himself as you progress in this book.

So this is what you need to do:

 a. Turn to the Word and open your bible at Genesis 1.
 b. Now you are going to do a study of your own on this chapter.
 c. With every single verse you read, I want you to visualize the creation as the Lord describes it.
 d. Work through the chapter slowly, making sure that you grasp each picture before moving on to the next.
 e. By the end of the chapter you should have a full overview of what the creation looked like from conception to birth!

As you do this, Word will begin sinking deep into your spirit. As you can see, feel, taste and smell the images that are being painted for you in this chapter, you will remember the Word, as never before. It will become real to you, and you will start feeling a stirring within, as the Word ministers to you.

You can apply this principle to any scripture, anywhere in the Word. For now, simply apply it to Genesis 1, until you feel comfortable with this form of study. Many people have learned to memorize the Word with their minds, but seldom gain from it in their spirits.

By visualizing the events, seeing each change and addition to the earth, you will see things in Genesis 1 you never noticed before. It is exciting to receive revelation from the Word for yourself and as you put this project to practice, the Holy Spirit will speak through scriptures to you more often.

EXERCISE: HEALING VS. PURGING DREAM

There are two dreams listed below. As you read through each one. You need to identify which is a healing dream and which is a purging dream.

DREAM 1

"I dreamed that I was trying to sleep and this person (who I really do not get on well with in real life) kept coming into my bedroom and interrupting my sleep. The more I kept telling him to get out, the more he ignored me.

I just got mad and the whole night I 'wrestled' with this person. We fought and yelled at one another. At one stage in the dream I actually got physical and tried to hit him.

In reality it seems so silly, but in this dream I was just so mad that I could have beaten him up! I woke up feeling rather tired after a full night of yelling and fighting. In reality I had been facing conflict with this person but was trying to bite my tongue and not cause any trouble."

IDENTIFY IT!

1. **What category of dream is this?**

    o   Healing Dream
    o   Purging Dream

2. **Why do you think it is this category of dream?**

    _____

    _____

    _____

    _____

DREAM 2

"I dreamed that I met up with an old boyfriend. In reality we had broken up badly and I was left with a lot of hurts after the break up. Even years later when I thought back on this person, I would get a knot in my stomach and feel like I had failed. I was bitter and it was a memory I did not want to face again.

Yet in this dream, he was being very friendly to me. In my dream he was washing my car and was joking around with me. He just did not seem like the same person. In my dream, we were just joking around like we had been friends for years. Then I woke up feeling like I had somehow left a load behind."

IDENTIFY IT!

3. **What category of dream is this?**

   o   Healing Dream
   o   Purging Dream

4. **Why do you think it is this category of dream?**

_____

_____

_____

_____

EXTRA NOTES:

_____

_____

_____

_____

_____

_____

_____

_____

_____

LESSON 02 – PROPHETIC DREAMS

Based on: *The Way of Dreams and Visions*, Chapter 2

INTERNAL DREAMS

As I already mentioned, all the symbols in these dreams are common to you. Dreams like this are a representation, telling you what is happening in your life right now, or something that happened in your past and is effecting you right now.

Have you ever cried out to the Lord, for the answer to something you are struggling with, only to have a clear dream that night? That internal dream is the answer to your prayer. The Lord is trying to shine the light on what is happening in your life right now.

THE "TELEPHONE DREAM"

Perhaps you have a dream where you are trying to call your dad, and you keep struggling to get through. This is a good example of an internal dream. If your relationship with your father is good, then it is likely that he represents the Lord in your dreams.

The dream would indicate then, that you are having a bit of a problem in getting through to the Lord right now. You are struggling to hear His voice or feel as if your prayers are not breaking through.

So remember this point – the internal dream represents what is happening in a person's life right now!

Now, knowing the interpretation for this dream is not good enough. There is no power in just knowing that there is a problem in your prayer life. No, it is only when you take some action that real ministry begins.

DREAMS ARE NOT FYI

So keep this in mind, as you start helping others understand their dreams and visions. They are not given by the Lord just "For Your Information." They are given for the purpose of being applied. Knowing you have a problem, puts the spotlight on your situation, but you need to DO something about it.

In this example, the first thing you need to do is identify why you are battling to get through to the Lord. Is there perhaps sin in your life that you feel guilty about? Have you allowed bitterness into your heart?

If someone shares their dream with you, do not finish up until you have shared the interpretation and action needed.

Joseph did not stand up and show Pharaoh how clever he was by only interpreting the dream. He went on to give direction as well. He told the king that it would be a pretty good idea to store up food for the seven years of plenty while the going was good. In the same way, an interpretation is empty without application.

Do not base your life on dreams, but use them as a tool to walk through the door to a broader revelation that will come from the Lord through other ways of hearing Him.

START HERE

Very often people desire their dreams to be external. It is easier for them to imagine that the person in their dream is the same as the person in real life, than to face the fact that a part of them needs to be looked at.

However, as an interpreter, trust me when I say that it is best that you start with interpreting a dream as internal FIRST! You cannot go wrong using the symbols in someone's dream and applying it to their lives and then following up with ministry.

It is only when you cannot interpret the dream at all as internal, that you look at interpreting it as external. If you have any doubt or you are unsure of a dream, rather lean towards interpreting it as internal. This will give you a direction to follow and still enable you to minister to that person.

INTERNAL PROPHETIC DREAMS

This dream type is not terribly different to the straight internal dream, and it can be a bit confusing at times to discern the difference.

While in both dreams you are the star of the show and the symbols are all about you, the internal prophetic has two distinct differences.

The first is that some of the symbols in the dream are not the same.

The other difference is that the interpretation of this dream relates to things in the future and not the present or past, like the internal dream.

Consider again, Paul who saw the Macedonian. The symbol was not familiar to him, but the interpretation indicated that this was something that would still happen. It was direction for the future.

Joseph is also a great example for this kind of dream. In his dream, he saw the twelve stars bow down to him. This was something that only happened in the future.

In *The Way of Dreams and Visions,* I go into a lot of detail about what an unfamiliar symbol is along with a bunch of other Scriptural examples. So I will not repeat myself here, but press forward with some more practical stuff on how to apply those principles!

What is so fantastic about the internal prophetic dream, is that God is giving direction for the future. Prophets especially operate in this dream category, but it is available to every believer.

The Lord desires to give every believer direction! He desires to be a part of their lives, if you would only open their eyes to what He is saying, you will give them so much hope!

So often, people think that they have to run to a prophet to hear the Lord for themselves. Little do they know that God is already speaking to them. It is for you to help them identify that and also teach them how to interpret their dreams for themselves.

We have not gotten into interpreting symbols just yet, but for now help them to categorize it! Is the message simple? Are they the star of the show? Are the symbols uncommon? Then the Lord is giving direction about their future!

THE WORD IS YOUR LIFELINE

In the internal dream, because all of the symbols are particular to just that person, you need to know a bit more about them before giving your interpretation. However, with the internal prophetic, a new set of rules applies.

Those unfamiliar symbols in the dream, will have their interpretation based in the Word! The Holy Spirit will never contradict Himself. He will always speak through the Word. Apostle Paul said to the early church to reject anyone who spoke against the gospel!

He said:

> *Galatians 1:8 But even if we, or an angel from heaven, preach any other gospel to you than what we have preached to you, let him be accursed.*

Those are some strong words! The Holy Spirit will always confirm the Word. He will not speak contrary to Himself. When He speaks to you in a dream or vision or any other way, He will speak to you through the types and shadows already in the Word.

For the most part, you will find that He will speak to you through the types and shadows in the Word that you are already familiar with. This is why it is important to be well fed with the Word – you give the Lord more to work with!

The great thing is, that if there is an unfamiliar symbol in your dream that you are not sure of, you can start digging through the Word and find it there. I have made that easy for you though and wrote the *Dreams and Visions Symbol Dictionary* to help you out with that! I did all of the studying for you!

A WORD OF CAUTION

It is dangerous to try and look in the world or in other religions for your answers! The Lord will speak through His Word and He will also speak through your own life experience. He will certainly not use an unknown demonic symbols to tell you of His love!

This is important to remember especially regarding experiences with angels and demons. If you want to make sure that you steer clear of deception, then remember that the Word is our foundation. I find it shocking sometimes to see people defending their revelations, simply because they have discovered that the symbol in their dream is from a demonic cult!

Simply because the New Age cults believe in female angels and you see one, certainly does not mean that God is speaking to you. Quite the contrary. It means that you have a contamination in your spirit and that the enemy is leading you astray.

Hopefully, I am helping you find some balance here. If you can base your revelation on the Word, and then on revelation that the Holy Spirit gives you, you will have balance. This will bring the conviction that is needed!

You are called to bring change to the body of Christ. You cannot bring that change though, unless you stand in power and in truth. The Lord is light, life, and love - you cannot stand in that if your entire purpose of interpreting dreams, is to look good.

No, we must speak the truth and stand in the light as He is in the light. Then you will stand in power. Then you will bring true change to God's people!

CONFRONTING THE PHARISEES

You will get many that will come to you and say, "I am a dreamer. That is how God uses me." They will then proceed to tell you all of their fantastic dreams. It will be clear that they do not want your interpretation, but have already decided in their minds what the dreams mean.

Ask yourself, "What is the purpose of all this?" How are those dreams ministering to the body of Christ? How have these dreams helped this person mature in their walk with the Lord?

If all the dream is doing is making *them* look good, then what is the purpose? The purpose of all the gifts and ministries is to bring the body of Christ to a place of unity and maturity.

So if those dreams are doing nothing but exalting the person bragging about them, what ministry is being accomplished? You will often be used of God to bring truth to this kind of person.

Just as Jesus was not afraid to confront the Pharisees, do not be surprised to find yourself in a situation where you have to shine the light.

He will use you to come with a sword, to bring division between the darkness and the Lord. You will be able to look objectively and say, "Yes, that dream is clearly of God" or "No, that is purely internal and for you." Perhaps you might be used of God to say, "I am afraid that dream has 'a spirit of divination' written all over it!"

I will be up front with you here and say that you will face that often. However, if you are armed with love and with the Word, you will be able to speak that truth. Those that really do love the Lord and want the truth will cling to it and be changed.

PEOPLE HUNGER FOR TRUTH

Not all the dream interpretations we receive are what we want to hear. However, if it is a revelation that you did not think of before, it is likely of the Lord! That is why it is called "revelation!" You did not think of it yourself before. However, that revelation will witness in your spirit.

It might not always be comfortable, but you will know it is the truth.

There are so few in the Church who are willing to stand up and give the truth. Why? It is because it is a tough job! Do not condemn them, but make your own choices. It is not easy to tell the truth when you are facing one rejection after the other. However, when you do find a leader that is not afraid to stand up in boldness, they gain your respect.

Remember this when you find yourself in a sticky situation. Sure, learn to share that truth with a bit of tact. However, share that truth! The people of God deserve no less.

QUESTIONS FOR REVIEW

1. Who is capable of having a prophetic dream?

   _____

   _____

2. How do you identify an internal dream?

   _____

   _____

   _____

3. What 2 categories of prophetic dreams were covered in this lesson?

   _____

   _____

   _____

4. How would you identify an internal prophetic dream?

   _____

   _____

   _____

5. Can you think of any other examples of internal prophetic dreams in Scripture?

_____

_____

_____

_____

_____

_____

PRACTICAL PROJECT

Write down an example of the most recent internal dream you have had. Dream:

_____

_____

_____

_____

_____

_____

_____

_____

_____

Taking your dream above, answer the following:

1. How did you identify this as an internal dream?

   _____
   _____
   _____
   _____
   _____

2. List all the characters and symbols that stood out in your dream. Then next to each character, make a summary of your relationship with that person in the natural and try to identify which part of you they could represent.

   SYMBOLS:
   _____
   _____
   _____
   _____
   _____
   _____
   _____
   _____
   _____

CHARACTER	SUMMARY OF RELATIONSHIP

As we continue, I will help you identify the characters and symbols in your dreams a little more easily, but the key for now, is to identify those characters that are often in your dreams. If you find yourself having a dream with symbols that you do not understand, look into the Word for your answers. Look up more examples of dreams in Scripture. Look up the words "Night" and "Vision", "Visions" and "Bed", "Dreams" and "Dream". You will be amazed to see how much the Lord used dreams to speak to His prophets through the ages!

EXERCISE: THE INTERNAL DREAM

Below is an example of an internal dream. Read the dream, then answer the questions.

> **THE AWARD**
>
> "I dreamt that I met up with an old boyfriend. In reality we had broken up badly and I was left with a lot of hurts after the break up. Even years later when I thought back on this person, I would get a knot in my stomach and feel like I had failed. I was bitter and it was a memory I did not want to face again.
>
> Yet in this dream he was being very friendly to me. In my dream he was washing my car and was joking around with me. He just did not seem like the same person. In my dream we were just joking around like we had been friends for years. Then I woke up feeling like I had somehow left a load behind."
>
>

IDENTIFY IT!

Use the principles you have learned so far and identify the following points from the given dream. (My own interpretation will be available at the back of the book so that you see if you received anything similar).

    a. Why would you say this is an internal dream? What identifies it as one?

_____

_____

_____

_____

_____

b. What were the characters and symbols in the dream?

_____
_____
_____

c. What did the characters and symbols represent in the dream?

_____
_____
_____
_____

INTERPRET IT!

So what do you feel the dream means? Write down your own interpretation and then compare it to my interpretation at the back of the book.

_____
_____
_____
_____
_____
_____
_____

EXTRA NOTES:

LESSON 03 – EXTERNAL PROPHETIC DREAMS

Based on: *The Way of Dreams and Visions*, Chapter 3 and 5

MOVE ON! THE MANNA IS GONE

You will get people that will bring their long list of dreams from years before. I have one message for people like this, "Move on!" You should be hearing something new from God every day! If you are still holding onto revelations from 15 years ago, then I question your relationship with the Lord right now!

This goes for your own spiritual walk. Are you still holding onto dreams and revelations you had gotten years back? Revelation is unfolding and progressive. If you keep looking back, you will keep hindering your progress forward!

There is a lot more that God has in store for you, but while you fill your arms with the little bit you had from the past, you will never get the full picture of what God had in mind.

When the children of Israel were in the wilderness, the Lord sent them manna. However, when they entered the Promised Land, that manna stopped. Why? They did not need it any longer because they had huge vines and fruit trees to eat from!

The Rhema Word of God is for a specific time and season and when it is fresh, it is delicious. However, just as leftover manna got worms and went rotten, in the same way, your revelations of the past quickly pass their expiry date!

What you have received so far in your ministry has been manna. However, God has so much more for you. So if the dreams stopped or you feel stuck, then it is time to let go! Let go of your visions and hopes of the past, and look forward to the Promised Land.

Sure you might have a Philistine or two to kick off it, but it will mean eating off the fat of that land. As you grow, those you minister to will grow as well. You will live what you will teach others – never forget that.

So if the manna is going stale or drying up, do not be discouraged. The Promised Land is ahead. It is time to mature in your walk as a believer.

You know when the disciples followed Jesus, they started out with the idea that He was going to defeat the Romans and restore Israel's supremacy. They had no idea what Jesus really came to do. It was only after He resurrected, and they experienced the power of the Holy Spirit that the bigger picture started to come together.

I bet when Peter was listening to Jesus preach and had his first conviction to follow, he did not know he would later be standing in a gentile's house proclaiming the gospel! The revelation was progressive, and God showed him what to do one step at a time.

It is the same with your spiritual walk. You do not have the full picture yet of how God wants to use you. Yet, you hold onto all of your old visions and pictures, instead of seeking God for new ones.

So do yourself a huge favor right now. Move on! Put down every vision and dream from your past. Let them settle back there and start looking forward. Seek God for new experiences, visions and dreams.

Then as you let that concept sink into your spirit, you will be able to teach others to do the same thing!

TAKING AWAY THAT STALE MANNA!

Do not be afraid to tell someone to let go of their old dreams, because holding onto them stops the Lord from giving them something new. How do they know that God is not standing there with a fresh vision and an invitation into something wonderful?

They have cried out to Him and He has answered. He has the Promised Land stretched out ahead of them, but they are too afraid to let go of that manna and eat the fruit. Right now, the Lord could have a new provision or ministry vision for them.

By not speaking out with the truth, you leave them on a spiritual plateau. So when someone comes to you with their dreams from years ago, tell them to put them on the backburner, because God has something new for them right now!

If that same person is trying to flow more in dreams, the reason that they might not be experiencing internal prophetic dreams is because they are looking back too much instead of looking forward!

If there was something in those dreams that God wants the person to hold onto, then He will give them another dream or revelation to confirm it.

TRUE LOVE WITH JESUS

The Lord Jesus wants to draw every believer into an intimate relationship with Him. However, if all they can talk about is the, "old days," that relationship will never grow. That would be like keeping old love letters. Imagine that I held onto every love letter that my husband gave me when we were dating.

What is more special? Hearing today that he loves me, or having to dig into those old letters to be reminded? It would be a sad state of affairs for my marriage if all I had to remember my husband's love by were some letters written years ago!

No, we know that even in marriage, that love is kept alive by working on your relationship daily. How different is this with the Lord? Why dig out the "old love letters" when you can hear the Lord say something sweet to you right now?

Sure our experiences with the Lord in the past were fantastic, but you cannot live off those your entire life! Without new experiences and revelations, our spirits dry up completely and our relationship with the Lord suffers.

INTRODUCING JESUS

As your dreams become clear, someone will start cropping up in your dreams that will be a picture of the Lord Jesus. This person will likely be your spouse, or perhaps your first love. Then when you dream of that person, you will know that this dream is a direct message from the Lord Jesus.

Isn't that something? Many believers are so hungry for this relationship with the Lord. They go around for years, feeling that they are not special enough for God to talk to them. They think that they must do something incredible, before they can have this intimacy that they crave.

You hold the power in your hands to change all of that. By helping them identify the symbol in their dreams that represents Jesus, you can let them know that Jesus is talking to them right now! Right in the privacy of their dreams, He is sending them love letters.

He is giving them a message meant only for their ears. You can start a fresh love affair with that person and Jesus, help them fall in love again with the one that saved them, and continues to set them free.

When they see this, it will draw them closer and closer to the Lord. They will feel important to Him. At first it might seem tough for you to confront people, who always want "super-duper" interpretations to their dreams, but in the end, it is worth it.

If you can break through their wrong thinking, you will be introducing Jesus to them. For the first time in their lives, they can truly have the intimacy with Jesus that they always craved. Right here, you will be making the Bride of Christ ready for her Groom.

QUESTIONS FOR REVIEW

1. What is the most marked difference between an internal and external dream?

   _____
   _____
   _____

2. What are the three kinds of recurring dreams?

   _____
   _____
   _____

3. For what purpose does the Holy Spirit give us prophetic dreams?

   _____
   _____
   _____

4. What must you do with an interpretation once you have an understanding of it?

   _____
   _____
   _____

5. Can you think of any other clear examples of external dreams in Scripture?

_____

_____

_____

_____

PRACTICAL PROJECT

1. Have you ever had an external dream? If so, write it down now for later study. Your own external dream:

_____

_____

_____

_____

_____

_____

_____

_____

_____

_____

2. **Do others come to you for help with their dreams and vision? If so, assess if you have learned how to apply the interpretation to their lives.**

_____

_____

_____

_____

_____

_____

_____

It is important to note that if the Lord is giving you an increasing amount of external dreams, that you could be moving in the prophetic ministry without being fully aware of it. Now would be the time to identify this gift in your life, and to look into what the Lord has for you.

EXERCISE

THE INTERNAL PROPHETIC DREAM

On the next page is an example of an internal prophetic dream. Read the dream, then answer the questions below.

> **EAGLES**
>
> "This dream was actually given to my nephew John, who is 20 years old and he shared this with us at the youth meeting we have at our home. (The kids are growing in the prophetic and are called very strongly in the area of prophetic evangelism). The dream began with him and myself looking into an eagle's nest which was covered. As he uncovered the nest we saw that three eagles were inside. The eagles were not quite fully grown and still had some growing to do before being ready to fly - that is they were fully developed and had full plumage etc. My words were to not touch them and to not cover them back up again. End of dream"
>
>

IDENTIFY IT!

Use the principles you have learned so far and identify the following points from the given dream. (My own interpretation will be available at the back of the book so that you see if you received anything similar).

  a. **Why would you say this is an internal prophetic dream? What identifies it as one?**

_____

_____

_____

_____

_____

_____

b. What were the characters and symbols in the dream?

_____

_____

_____

_____

c. What did the characters and symbols represent in the dream?

_____

_____

_____

_____

INTERPRET IT!

Now put it all together and write down your interpretation. Then compare it to mine at the back of the book. Remember to allow the Holy Spirit to give revelation through you. This is not a "mind" exercise. This is rather a spiritual exercise to stir the gifts within you.

_____

_____

_____

_____

EXTRA NOTES:

Lesson 04 - Five P's In Dream Interpretation

Based on: *The Way of Dreams and Visions*, Chapter 3 and 4

DUMPING THE "SUPER-DUPER"

I think that when it comes to dream interpretation, people are so busy looking for the dramatic experiences and messages, that they miss them when they really come. Because they want their dreams to apply to the Church, or to have some incredible bearing on their life, that they do not take the time to identify their internal dreams.

The crazy thing is, that if they only took the time to look at those simple internal and internal prophetic dreams, that they would see that they are in fact getting incredible revelation.

It might not be the revelation they want to get, but that is why God holds the earth in His hand and not us! If you can help God's people, to come down a little and let go of the idea of having incredible "earth-shaking" dream experiences, they will tap into the truth.

When they let go of trying to be super spiritual, they will discover a sweet truth. They will see that God has been telling them secrets all along. They have just not been listening.

Help God's people to identify their internal and internal prophetic dreams. Show them that Jesus has been speaking to them all along. You would have walked them to the door, and used your key to unlock it. Then you can stand and watch, knowing that you accomplished what Jesus sent you to do.

EXTERNAL PROPHETIC DREAM

This category of dream is more of the realm of the prophet and apostle. In this dream, you are not the star of it. In this dream, you are sitting on the outside watching the actions. It feels a lot like watching a movie.

A dream like this does not usually relate to you directly, although it can if the events indicate something you are involved in. For example, you could have an external dream where the Lord is giving you direction for a ministry that you are working with.

As a prophet you really need to learn to identify this dream correctly, so that you can apply the interpretation of this dream correctly. Remember how I said before that a dream is useless unless the interpretation is applied?

Well this is true, of this dream type even more! Often this kind of dream is a call to intercession. So do not think that if you have this kind of dream often that it means you need to share it with everyone. No, you will need to use a bit of wisdom here.

The most confusing thing about this dream, is that often you will still dream of people you are familiar with. Although this is not a hard and fast rule, even in this dream, the person in it is not necessarily the person in real life!

That person is likely symbolic of something specific. Say for example you dream of the President. Now this does not mean that your dream is for the President. Instead, he is a picture of the country as a whole. He might even be a picture of the world system.

The Lord speaks in types and shadows especially in dreams. If you have an external dream that someone dies, it does not mean they will actually die! That person might represent a ministry or a group, in which case the Lord is saying that He is going to dissolve that group or bring that ministry to a spiritual death.

If you see a destructive hurricane sweeping across a familiar landscape, do not jump up and tell everyone that God is going to destroy that country, and judge them by wiping them out with a hurricane!

No! The Lord is showing you that spiritual attack is coming. He might even be showing you, that He is going to remove the old so that He can do something new. He might be revealing that He, is about to bring about some major change in the church in that region – a shake up!

A hurricane can mean very many things, so use wisdom, and realize that it is symbolic. Please do not go out and dig a shelter in your backyard. Not only will you lose credibility with other believers, but your chance of witnessing to your neighbors just got blown out of the water!

Your dream is not about what is going to happen, but what you plan to do about it!

So what does it mean if you dream of people that you are familiar with, but the dream is clearly internal? Well that you need to assess for yourself. For example, when I used to dream of my stepmother, I knew that the Lord was speaking to me of the Church.

So if I saw her being attacked or receiving something new and the dream was external, I knew that God was saying He was about to do something in the Church. It is then for me to see what part He wants me to play in it, and how He wants me to pray.

Could you imagine, if I had an external dream of my stepmother coming under attack and I run off and tell her, "Watch out! You are in danger! Someone is going to attack you!" It would be a disaster! Not only would I produce fear, but I would be very wrong.

I would also have missed out on the opportunity to be involved in what God wanted me to do in His Church. Unfortunately, this happens a lot when believers are not sure on how to interpret dreams, which is why you are called to bring some balance.

So when someone comes to you panicking because they had a dream like that, you can put them at ease.

"No, the world is not coming to an end."

"No, your mother is not going to die."

"No, your husband is not going to leave you for another woman…"

STAY ON THE SAFE SIDE

Now I am not going to make it a hard and fast rule, and say that every single person in your external dream is symbolic only. It could well be, that the person really does represent themselves. However, you cannot go wrong interpreting that dream, using that person as a symbol only.

If you really cannot find an interpretation taking that route, then as a last resort consider that the person might actually speak of themselves.

I had something like that happen to me once. I had asked the Lord where a specific relationship was going with some folks we had met and ministered to. I had a clear external dream where the person turned their backs on us and showed a bad attitude.

I tried to interpret it internally, but the interpretation only came to light years later when they did what I had seen them do in the dream. The Lord was preparing our hearts and trying to give us wisdom on how to handle the situation.

If this does happen to you, let me give you a word of caution again. Do not run off with that revelation. Sit on it for a bit and ask the Lord for revelation. Journal and ask the Lord to clarify what He wants you to do. Once you have that confirmation and you know what God wants, then you can act.

So no hard and fast rules here. In the old days when I was the fiery "black and white" prophet, I left no room for error. However, having walked this road a little, I have come to believe that the Lord often likes to make the rules to break them!

Do not tell God how He should speak to you. Only be aware of the principles, and then allow the Holy Spirit to give you revelation through those principles.

I am sharing many different principles with you here, but more importantly I hope that I can impart to you revelation and wisdom. Without wisdom, none of these principles will do you any good, and that wisdom comes from the Holy Spirit.

So above all else, as you continue here with me, keep your heart open and be aware of the anointing you are receiving. Allow the Holy Spirit to teach you through these principles, and along with the knowledge will come the wisdom you need to apply that knowledge.

TWO PRINCIPLES TO LIVE BY

Now you will get some crazy dreams coming your way! Just remember these two simple facts and you cannot go wrong:

1. Categorize the dream correctly
2. All people, places and objects are symbolic

These two principles bring faith, hope and love. You can do that! Whether you are new to your prophetic walk, or you have been along this road for years, bring balance with these two principles and you have done most of your job.

Of course that is not all of it. You need to move onto identifying symbols and also onto applying that interpretation.

QUESTIONS FOR REVIEW

1. **What are the 5 p's of prayer?**

_____

_____

_____

_____

_____

_____

2. Can you recall ever having a dream where you woke up praising the lord?

_____

_____

_____

3. Why is it vital that you speak out and proclaim the revelation you receive in a dream?

_____

_____

_____

4. What are the three forces that are ultimately the purpose of every revelation?

_____

_____

_____

5. What is the purpose of a warning dream?

_____

_____

_____

_____

6. **Have you ever ministered and given a revelation of hope?**

_____

_____

_____

PRACTICAL PROJECT

Do you desire to have the wisdom to interpret revelation from dreams and visions? You can have this desire fulfilled. The Word says that if any man lacks wisdom, that He asks of God and God who gives to all men liberally will give him that wisdom! Reach out right now and ask the Lord, by His Word for that spirit of wisdom and revelation.

1. Now take a pen and paper in hand and I would like you to take one of the dreams you have documented so far and I want you to write the first impressions that come to your mind.

   Find a place that is quiet and where you are not distracted. Without trying to delve into the characters just yet, write down your impressions of how you felt in the dream and upon waking up. Document any events from the past that suddenly came back to your memory after the dream.

2. Now as you write, pictures will come to mind. Certain events will come to mind and specific people might even come to mind. Your dream may also begin to come back to you in a greater clarity. Simply write down the pictures you see. Do not try to interpret them yet, as you are learning how to flow from your spirit first.

   The interpretations will come soon enough. As you just let the words bubble up from within, you will find that the pictures will come faster and the emotions will also come in line.

   You will also note that the pictures you are seeing will form a pattern and line up with one another. You will begin seeing a common element.

IMPRESSIONS OF DREAM:

_____
_____
_____
_____
_____
_____
_____
_____
_____
_____
_____
_____
_____
_____
_____
_____
_____

Well done! You have just journaled your first dream. This is the starting point in interpreting any dream and as you continue to learn how to let the interpretation flow from your spirit, you will find the revelations will increase. This is the most powerful way to begin interpreting your dreams, and if you would put time aside each day to just write and let those words and pictures bubble from your spirit, you will begin to see and hear the Lord's will for you.

EXERCISE

EXTERNAL PROPHETIC DREAM - THE WARNING DREAM

Below is an example of a warning dream. These dreams always fall into the category of prophetic. Note that the dream does not induce fear, but rather faith and a positive move to action.

CRACKED FOUNDATION

"I dreamed that I was observing the inside of a house. There was no one else in the dream. It seemed as though I was not interacting with what was happening in the scenes, just observing. I heard a loud and sharp sound that happened quickly - it was actually an earthquake, but the movement was just one quick and strong jolt.

I looked at the wall/ceiling area in front of me and saw a horizontal crack along the joining area where the wall and ceiling met. Then I looked to the left and saw a large gaping hole that was in the ceiling... the wood framing and insulation in the ceiling and wall areas were now exposed.

I remember saying: "My mother's house has been damaged." (But this place was not actually my mother's house). I then remember looking at a lower level of this house and saw that the foundational walls were cracked so severely that the house was not safe to inhabit. I determined that the house must therefore be torn down and cleared away, and a new house should then be built, from the foundation up."

IDENTIFY IT!

Use the principles you have learned so far and identify the following points from the given dream. (My own interpretation will be available at the back of the book so that you see if you received anything similar).

a. Why would you say this is an external prophetic dream? What identifies it as one?

___

b. What were the characters and symbols in the dream?

___

c. What did the characters and symbols represent?

___

INTERPRET IT!

Now put these thoughts together and do a bit of searching in the Word for yourself on "foundations" and the "house of the Lord". Now write down your interpretation of this dream, then compare it to the interpretation I offered afterwards.

_____

_____

_____

_____

_____

_____

_____

_____

GROUP PROJECT: TAKING YOUR DREAMS APART

This project is perfect for small groups. For this project to be effective, divide everyone into groups of 5 people. We suggesting putting couples and close friends into separate groups for this project to be effective.

1. **Ask each student to think of a dream that they had recently.**

2. **Now going through the project, get each one to document their dream using the points provided.**

3. **Then get each student to read all points except their conclusions and final interpretation.**

4. **Get each student to share what they think the interpretation of the dream is.**

5. **Conclude the final interpretation yourself.**

It is often easier to interpret for others than for yourself. Again, this gives your students the opportunity to practice the principles in a safe environment.

EXTRA NOTES

PART 02

VISIONS: YOUR SECRET CONVERSATION WITH GOD

PART 02 – VISIONS: YOUR SECRET CONVERSATION WITH GOD

> **KEY PRINCIPLE**
>
> Prophetic visions are pictorial impressions that come to your mind from your spirit.

LESSON 05 - VISIONS: YOUR SECRET CONVERSATION WITH GOD

Based on: *The Way of Dreams and Visions*, Chapter 6

VISIONS

Visions are the language of God. Although it is possible for you to receive revelation via your other senses, receiving via vision is still the most common way in which you will receive revelation from the Lord.

Why are visions so powerful? Well think about it. What do you remember the most - what you did last week or the movie you watched ten years ago? Pictures make an impression on your mind. They stay with you.

When Jesus walked the earth, He spoke in pictures all the time. All of his parables were pictures. In fact, if you really want to see what part visions play in your spiritual walk, just take a look at this Scripture…

> *John 5:19 Then Jesus answered and said to them, "Most assuredly, I say to you, the Son can do nothing of Himself, but what He sees the Father do; for whatever He does, the Son also does in like manner."*

Jesus just says it so plainly here! He did only what He saw His father do. If ever you wanted to find someone in Scripture who literally lived in the realm of the Spirit, it was Jesus! He was in continual fellowship with the Father and kept His spiritual eyes and ears open to know which step to take, and which word to speak. This means that when Jesus raised Lazarus from the dead, He saw the Father show Him what to do first! It does not get any easier than that.

One afternoon we had a family lunch. It was common during a family get together like this, for there to be a lot of talking, eating, and laughing. We had put my daughter, Rebekah (still a toddler at this time) in her high chair as usual.

She did not eat with us, but had come to enjoy just sitting and watching. During the meal someone was relating a funny event to us, and at the end of it we all broke into laughter. Right in the middle of it came a high-pitched chuckle from the corner.

Beaming from ear to ear and laughing in a put on "laugh," Ruby imitated our laughter. She did not know what was so funny. In fact, she did not understand a word of it! She knew only one thing, "I see them laugh, so therefore now is the time to laugh!"

Learning to walk in your calling is as simple as watching the Lord and copying Him. You might not understand at first why you are doing what you are doing. You might not even understand the message at first, but the more you participate and laugh like you see the father laugh, so to speak, the more you will begin to flow in the pirit.

RECEIVING VISIONS

I will not go into detail here on how to receive a vision, because I have already covered that in *The Way of Dreams and Visions: Your Secret Conversation with God*. At this stage however, you should be familiar with receiving revelation via visions. So, I am going to point out some things for you to keep in mind, and also some suggestions on how to take the world of visions, and make them a springboard to revelation in your walk with God.

If you are familiar with the move of the Spirit and have been Spirit-filled for some time, then when you first start out receiving visions you might just see quick flashes that come every now and again. The visions you receive from the Lord will nudge and come back to you several times. They do not push, nor do they demand attention. Often the vision will be accompanied with that familiar feeling of butterflies in your stomach, which lets you know that the Holy Spirit is moving upon you.

THE STILL SMALL VOICE

What you are likely to find as you continue in your walk, is that the visions and revelation you receive begin to tone down and become more gentle over time. When you first begin hearing from the Lord, your emotions are high, the visions are strong and the Holy Spirit literally has to slay you in the Spirit, so that you know, "Ok, the Lord is talking to me now."

However, as you learn to identify His voice for yourself, He does not need to shout anymore. In fact, if you once experienced strong revelations and they have calmed down, do not panic! It does not mean that you are losing your gifts, it simply means that the Lord does not need to shout at you to get your attention anymore, because you can hear the gentle whisper of His voice.

As you remove any junk from your mind that might be blocking you from hearing the voice of the Lord, the revelation you receive will become more clear, but less "loud" and obvious. The Lord will speak more with impressions and "gut feelings" and less with overwhelming emotion.

THE SIGN OF MATURITY

This is a sign of maturity, and I think that if I had to use an example from the Word to depict this, I would use Elijah. Just take a look how he calmed down! We first see Elijah as he storms into the presence of Ahab, and declares that there will be no rain. Miracles follow and later you see him calling fire from heaven to consume the sacrifice in the sight of the priests of Baal.

But further down the road look at what Elijah discovers...

> *1 Kings 19:11 Then He said, "Go out, and stand on the mountain before the Lord." And behold, the Lord passed by, and a great and strong wind tore into the mountains and broke the rocks in pieces before the Lord, but the Lord was not in the wind; and after the wind an earthquake, but the Lord was not in the earthquake;*
>
> *12 and after the earthquake a fire, but the Lord was not in the fire; and after the fire a still small voice.*
>
> *13 So it was, when Elijah heard it, that he wrapped his face in his mantle and went out and stood in the entrance of the cave. Suddenly a voice came to him, and said, "What are you doing here, Elijah?*

Now Elijah had known the Lord's voice in the fire, and the mighty rushing wind. He had seen the Lord bring a storm upon the land, and he felt the power as he outran the chariot of Ahab, but what happens here? Elijah discovers that the voice of God is heard in the still small voice. It is here that Elijah begins to know the Lord in a new way.

Elisha, his disciple, learned the same lesson. Elisha begins his ministry by hitting the waters of the Jordan and yelling into the heavens, "Where is the Lord God of Elijah?" So dynamic! So powerful! Yet take a look at him years later and you will find Elisha sitting quite casually as a whole host of soldiers surround his house. This time his servant is panicking. Where is the great revelation now? Where is the dynamic shouting and seeking of signs?

Sounding almost bored, Elisha turns to his servant and says:

> *2 Kings 6:16 So he answered, "Do not fear, for those who are with us are more than those who are with them."*
>
> *17 And Elisha prayed, and said, "Lord, I pray, open his eyes that he may see." Then the Lord opened the eyes of the young man, and he saw. And behold, the mountain was full of horses and chariots of fire all around Elisha.*

Elisha then goes on to pray (notice how relaxed and calm he sounds here!)

> *2 Kings 6:18 So when the Syrians came down to him, Elisha prayed to the Lord, and said, "Strike this people, I pray, with blindness." And He struck them with blindness according to the word of Elisha.*

How had things changed now? Elisha no longer needed to have "super-duper" revelation to move mountains. He knew how to see and hear the Lord's gentle voice and he simply acted on what he saw.

Now if the visions you are seeing are not clear and you are not sure if what you are seeing is just your own mind or from the Lord, then ask the Lord for confirmation. The Word says that if you ask your Father for a fish that He will not give you a stone, and if you ask Him for bread He will not give you a scorpion. If you ask the Lord to clarify and to confirm what you are seeing, He will raise up others to confirm or He will give you another vision to clarify. Just press on and continue asking the Lord to speak to you through visions.

Before you know it, visions will be a part of your daily walk and you will wonder how you lived without their ever-present influence in your life.

QUESTIONS FOR REVIEW

1. What is the spirit of wisdom and revelation?

___

___

___

___

___

2. Who is able to have a vision?

_____

_____

_____

3. What is the purpose of any revelation?

_____

_____

_____

_____

_____

PRACTICAL PROJECT: RECEIVING FROM THE LORD

Do you earnestly desire to have visions? If so I would encourage you right now to stop what you are doing and to ask the Lord for this gift. Request it in all earnestness and then see Him giving it to you. It is like a big present neatly wrapped, with a ribbon around it. As He puts this gift in your hands, know that He has granted your request. The Lord will not withhold the Holy Spirit from any of His children that ask. He wants to grant you your hearts desire, so reach out now and begin to discover the secrets He has put aside for you!

Now I want you to meditate on these scriptures I have listed below and memorize them. Write them on a card. On the one side of your flash card put the scripture text, on the other side put the reference. Then memorize them throughout the day. Seeing if you can remember the reference for the text and the text for the reference.

As these scriptures sink deep into your spirit, you will find a new life and a new understanding of how the spiritual gifts come to you. However, do not stop here! You should be memorizing the Word all the time to ensure that the revelation the Lord gives you, flows freely and that you have an understanding of what He has to say. For the Word interprets the Spirit – without it you have no track to run on when it comes to interpretation.

SCRIPTURES TO MEMORIZE:

> ***Ephesians 1:17*** *That the God of our Lord Jesus Christ, the Father of glory, may give to you the spirit of wisdom and revelation in the knowledge of Him.*
>
> ***1 Corinthians 14:1*** *Pursue love, and desire spiritual gifts, but especially that you may prophesy.*
>
> ***Luke 11:13*** *If you then, being evil, know how to give good gifts to your children, how much more will your heavenly Father give the Holy Spirit to those who ask Him!*
>
> ***1 Corinthians 12:6*** *And there are diversities of activities, but it is the same God who works all in all.*
>
> *7 But the manifestation of the Spirit is given to each one for the profit of all.*

EXERCISE: TAPPING YOUR INNER RESOURCES

It is vital that you learn to tap what the Lord has put within your spirit, if you desire to hear His voice and move into that wonderful relationship available to us. If we look at the natural, what would you say is the best way to get to know someone? When you first met your spouse or fiancé what did you spend a lot of your time doing?

Well if I go back to my engagement to Craig, I remember us talking for many hours about everything you could think of! Nights seemed to just slip by into early morning as we found out more about each other. The more we spoke the more we discovered how much we had in common! We dreamed about what it would be like when we got married one day and what we would do. We never seemed to run out of things to learn about each other and each day was a new adventure!

Well getting to know the Lord Jesus is just like that! Only you can never run out of things to find out about Him! On top of that, He never tires of listening to you and knowing all He can about you! It is a love affair made in heaven! It is within your reach if you have that desire in your heart. So just as in the natural you spent hours talking and sharing, so this week I want you to spend time every day talking to the Lord!

HERE ARE SOME GUIDELINES TO FOLLOW:

   a. Find a quiet spot where you will not be interrupted. Unhook the phone if you have to!

   b. Take out a notebook and pour your heart out on it to the Lord. Speak to Him as if He was standing right in front of you. Do not be afraid to say exactly what is on your heart. He is faithful and has tremendous patience! So say everything you always wanted to say.

   c. Then as you finish pouring out your heart, quiet your spirit and wait for Him to speak back.

   d. He might speak in visions, in words, or just in impressions.

   e. The key here is to just pour out as you feel the surge within. If you see a picture, then just describe it.

   f. Do this every single day for a week. Twice daily if you can. I guarantee that by the end of the week you will already be beginning to walk in a closer relationship with the Lord!

Journaling is very much like speaking in tongues! You might need to make the effort with the first few words, but as the Holy Spirit takes over your tongue, there is no stopping Him! Journaling is the same, you might feel like you are making up the first few words or sentences, but as you continue to write, you will find words and pictures coming to you that you did not originate.

EXTRA NOTES

_____

_____

_____

_____

_____

Lesson 06 - Three Spiritual Functions

Based on: *The Way of Dreams and Visions*, Chapter 6 and 7

> *1 Thessalonians 5:23 And the very God of peace sanctify you wholly; and [I pray God] your whole spirit and soul and body be preserved blameless unto the coming of our Lord Jesus Christ. (KJV)*

This passage speaks of getting your spirit, soul, and body in line. There is no greater illustration of this in the Word than that of the tabernacle.

As you well know, the Word says that we are the temple of the Lord. This again confirms the fact that we are tripartite - because the temple had three distinct parts!

Let us look at each of these right now.

1. THE OUTER COURT – THE BODY

The first part of the Tabernacle was called the Outer Court. This is the part where any Israelite could come and bring their offerings to God. It was public, just as our bodies are public. It is the part of ourselves that shows the world who we are. It is what people first come to know as "us." However, this is only the start of any relationship.

Just as the Outer Court had clear functions – so do our bodies! In fact, if you had to sum up three natural functions of the body they would read like this key principle.

> **KEY PRINCIPLE**
>
> The functions of the body are:
>
> a. Nourishment
> b. Self Defense
> c. Reproduction

As the saying goes, "beauty is only skin deep" and so who we truly are is not reflected by how we look. Who we are lies in the seat of our soul!

2. THE INNER COURT/HOLY PLACE – THE SOUL

The second part of the Tabernacle was called the Inner Court or Holy Place. It was an area that only the priests could enter. Not just any Joe could walk in and do what they wanted. Even then the priests had to fulfill certain conditions before they could enter. They had to be ceremonially clean and had to wash before coming into this part of the Temple.

This is a fantastic picture of our souls, because this part shows who we are, and we restrict it to a certain few. Only those who are allowed close enough, truly get to know you. Here lies your mind, emotions, and will. Your soul is a bridge between your body and spirit. It is also the control tower that decides what it will let through.

Your soul is where you make the decision to obey your spirit, or to follow after the things of your flesh! The Scripture says that we are to diffuse the fragrance of Christ wherever we go - it is no surprise then, that the altar of incense could be found in the Holy Place. What we say, do or think, reflects what is in our spirits.

Either this can be a fragrance that diffuses Christ, or it can be the smell of rotting flesh. Either way, your soul makes these choices. (2 Corinthians 2:14)

Just like your body, your soul also has three distinct functions. Make a good note of them because I will refer to them very often throughout this book.

> **KEY PRINCIPLE**
>
> The functions of the soul are:
>
> a. Mind
> b. Emotions
> c. Will

3. THE HOLY OF HOLIES – THE SPIRIT

The Holy of Holies of the Tabernacle contained the Ark of the Covenant and only the High Priest could enter into it. It was the most holy place and it was where God sat upon His "throne." It was where the cloud rested. It is a beautiful picture of our human spirits and what God intended for us.

As a human being, God has given us as a spirit. However, as a Christian, your spirit becomes His throne! It becomes a place where the cloud of God rests. Understanding this concept makes you realize everything that is available to us as believers!

Not only do we have a spirit that can communicate with the Lord, but it is a place that contains His power as well. What miracles are you looking for today? Do you realize that Jesus is on your throne? He is seated in your spirit, and He has brought along with Him all the authority that Adam lost.

It means that at the name of Jesus every demon must bow! When you realize that the power of God is not something you have to run after, but something that is within you, it brings you peace and builds your faith.

You already know the functions of both the body and soul – but how about the spirit?

> **KEY PRINCIPLE**
>
> The functions of the spirit are:
>
> a. Intuition
> b. Communion
> c. Spirit of Wisdom/Foreknowledge

As you get a full picture of how God made you, you will also start to see the vast authority you now have in Christ. You do not need to wander through life, waiting for something to happen to you. Rather, you can know who you are, know who the Lord is, and rest in that power!

THE FUNCTIONS OF THE SOUL

You face stimuli every day. If you think back on your day so far, you might remember the taste of your bagel. Perhaps you remember the smell of cigarette smoke, on the way to your office, and the sound of honking of horns as you got stuck in traffic.

Everywhere you go, stimuli are being fed into your spirit via your soul. Now although a lot of that can be negative, a lot is positive as well. For example, each time you read the Word or experience the anointing, you are feeding it into your spirit.

> **KEY PRINCIPLE**
>
> So the pattern looks a little bit like this:
>
> Sensation on the body > Creates a thought/emotion in the soul > Leaves an impression on your spirit!

YOUR FIVE SENSES

Everything you see, taste, touch, smell or hear through your body has an effect on your soul! It affects your mind (the way you think). It makes you feel something in your emotions, or it drives your will to action.

This is the way God created us, and it helps us sort through everything we receive. We accumulate all the information around us through the five senses in our bodies. It is our soul that makes sense of it so that we can "get a handle" on everything that is going on around us.

It is our God-given ability that assists us in learning. A baby falls, and the pain compels him to balance better. The same baby tastes candy for the first time, and it compels him to ask for more… bit by bit our soul makes sense of everything we experience throughout our day.

From there, it creates templates for life. Now use this in a spiritual context and you have a bomb of potential! Each time you allow yourself to experience things in the Word and spirit of God, you feed that influence into your soul, creating a solid foundation in your spirit!

This is what Paul meant when he said,

> *Romans 12:2 And do not be conformed to this world, but be transformed by the renewing of your mind, that you may prove what is that good and acceptable and perfect will of God.*

By allowing the spirit of God to dominate your senses, it will change the way you think, allowing you to know the will of God!

That is why I teach the prophets to meditate on the Word and to visualize it – so that they can create good spiritual templates for life.

WHEN GOD TALKS BACK

Now when God talks back to you, He is going to use the same modus operandi. He is going to use your mind, emotions and will, to get His message across to you. Just like the world imposes its will on you daily, from your body inwards, the Lord will speak gently to you in your spirit. What He says in your spirit can then be expressed outward.

The same way our soul comprehends stimuli through the five senses fed through our bodies - the Lord will speak through those same senses again from the spirit! He will feed you information that you can taste, touch, smell, feel or hear!

Think about that for a moment. You might be in a church meeting when you will suddenly feel a deep peace enter your heart. You might even taste or smell something in the Spirit. Sometimes these impressions are so strong that you might even smell or taste it physically!

THE MIND – A ONE WAY STREET

Now, it is important to keep in mind that you cannot take stimuli in and express them outwardly all at the same time. Your mind tends to be a one-way street. Have you noticed how hard it is to hear the gentle promptings from the Spirit, when you are distracted with noise around you?

That is why it is important to take time to feed into your spirit and just as important, to stop for a moment, to listen to what the Lord is saying deep inside of you. When you need to hear the Lord, try cutting out the distractions around you. Turn down the music and shut out the noise.

If you feel uncomfortable, find a better chair to sit on.

Quiet those senses of yours for a little while, so that you can feel the Lord trying to express Himself through them from within.

QUESTIONS FOR REVIEW

1. **What is a vision?**

_____

_____

_____

2. Why is it easier to receive revelation via vision, in comparison to the other four senses?

_____

_____

_____

3. A vision is imprinted on your mind, but where does that vision actually come from?

_____

_____

_____

4. What are the three natural functions of the human spirit?

_____

_____

_____

_____

PRACTICAL PROJECT

RECEIVING VISIONS

In the previous *Practical Project*, you reached out in faith and asked the Lord for the ability to have visions and you meditated on the Word. Like anything we receive from the hand of the Lord, you received that gift by faith! The Lord is speaking to you all the time and even though you may not know it, many visions have been coming up from your spirit from as early as the day of your salvation! You just never stopped to listen or "look" before.

So today you are going to stop and look in the Spirit. Find a quiet spot and make sure that you are at ease. If you feel upset or stressed out, then perhaps it would be better for you to wait until you feel more at peace before going on.

1. Spend some time in the presence of the Lord for a while. Praise is a wonderful way to touch the Lord, so if you can, sing or play an instrument. It worked for Elisha! If you cannot sing, then put on an anointed CD that brings you into the presence of the Lord.

2. Try not to be distracted by the circumstance that surrounds you. Put your eyes on Jesus and give Him all your attention. He is there, just take the time now to touch Him!

3. Now close your eyes and identify any pictures you see in your mind. You might think that they are your imagination and at first the images that come to you could be the movie you saw last night! But continue worshiping and praising the Lord until that 'junk' clears.

4. As more pictures come to your mind, write them down.

SOME HELPFUL HINTS:

- If you see symbols that you are unfamiliar with, go to the Word and look them up.

- It would also be a good idea for you to submit these to someone that you know moves in visions so that they might judge it for you and help you with their interpretation.

- If you just cannot seem to break through in the Spirit, it is likely that your inner man is blocked by all the "junk" it has been fed over the years. The best way to break through is to speak in tongues. When we train the prophets, the first project we give them is to speak in tongues for an hour! It might take some effort, but as you speak in tongues and clear away all that junk, a clear stream will come out!

- As you become accustomed to identifying these pictures that come to you, you will begin to flow very comfortably in visions and their interpretations. All is available to you in the Lord Jesus if you desire it!

PICTURES:

EXERCISE

Can you identify the following functions of your human spirit?

- Intuition
- Inner/Spiritual Wisdom
- Communion

To do this, you would need to think back on events and experiences you have had where these functions took place. So fill in the table on the next page and list what comes to your mind under those three headings.

Intuition: A sense of knowing relating to the present. A deep knowing of things positive or negative. It is what they call a 'gut feel'. Where you just knew that you should not go in a certain direction. Where you just knew within, that you should be going in a different direction.

Inner/Spiritual Wisdom: A sense of knowing relating to the future. Where you just knew that events were going to occur. These events do not have to be something supernatural. Just simple things like knowing the phone was going to ring, knowing that things were just going to work out in your circumstance.

Communication: You just seem to know and sense what others around you are feeling. You know when they are upset or when they are hiding something inside. You can sense when you have said something and it was not well received. Or on the opposite end you can feel when you are welcomed when you say something.

Now keep in mind that these are *natural* functions of the human spirit. Every human has the capacity for these and unfortunately the enemy has used these very functions to lead many into deception and into occult activity. As you can identify how these functions operate in your own life, you will also learn how to discern the spirit on revelation and judge it by the Word.

These functions are NOT the gifts of the Spirit! The gifts of the Spirit are the supernatural ability to hear from the Lord via our recreated spirits. That is why they are called gifts… we never had them before.

INTUITION:

INNER WISDOM:

COMMUNICATION:

EXTRA NOTES

Lesson 07 – Spiritual Fruit

Based on: *The Way of Dreams and Visions*, Chapter 7 and 8

THE LOVE FOUNDATION

I always thought that when a house advertised "natural stone" floors that this was a tremendous benefit. That was until we actually lived in a house with natural stone floors.

It turns out, that if you do not use the right detergent on these floors, you can strip their protective coating. Once that coating is gone, the natural stone is extremely porous and wears down with just simple use.

Only once huge cracks and holes started developing in these 'top of the line' floor tiles, did we find out our mistake. The hunt began as we started trying to figure out how to fix these floors.

Finally, the cheapest and easiest solution was to repair them ourselves.

So picture it if you may. Craig, myself and our team, sprawled over various parts of the flooring, looking for cracks, filling each one meticulously with a filler.

Hours turned into days and after some serious backbreaking, filling, scraping and buffing, the holes were filled.

But the job was still not complete. After all that hard work, the most important was still to come. We had to reapply that sealant. Only then would our hard work pay off.

And you thought the life of an apostle was all glamour…

Somewhere between accidentally spilling filler all over my pants and trying to keep my son from "helping out," I realized what a perfect illustration this was of good, solid leadership.

THE STUFF THAT KEEPS IT TOGETHER

> *Hebrews 10:16 This is the covenant that I will make with them after those days, says the Lord: I will put My **laws** into their **hearts**, and in their minds I will write them*

The principles that God has put into your heart has made a solid foundation. All of the teaching you have received here. All of the lessons you have learned through life. They are a foundation that will keep you strong for years to come.

However, let us not forget the sealant. There is a very special force, that we have as believers that keeps all of this together and without it, your foundation is in threat of developing some serious cracks.

THE SEALANT

So what is it that keeps your foundation in good shape? Can you guess?

> *1 Peter 1:22 Since you have purified your souls in obeying the truth through the Spirit in sincere love of the brethren,* **love** *one another fervently with a pure* **heart**,

It is the agape love of the Lord that seals your foundation. It is the ultimate force that keeps everything together.

You can have all the right principles and know the Word from beginning to end. However, without the love of the Lord covering you, you are nothing but a clanging symbol.

It is truly the love of the Lord that is your foundation. As you make this foundation firm, you will have a starting point to build the Kingdom of God.

But it is so easy to become imbalanced. You can concentrate so much on study and on understanding, that you forget the wisdom of walking in love.

Without love, your knowledge is empty. Without love, you have a weak and porous foundation.

Without love, your knowledge is dry bread, lacking the vitamins to bring life to those that hear it.

Ezekiel knew it well when he spoke about dead and dry bones. Without love, your life has no shine to it. It is empty and you have nothing to pour out to the Church.

HOW YOUR LOVE ERODES

If only we had known about that detergent! However, it was just too late when we discovered our mistake. Unfortunately, it is the same when it comes to your own foundation.

Life comes at you like a hurricane and before you know it, all the love and peace you had disappears in the storm cloud.

Let's look at some of the things that are a serious threat to keeping your heart sealed in His love.

1. PEOPLE

I heard a saying once that goes like this,

"Life would be wonderful, if it were not for other people"

You can wake up motivated and ready to conquer the world, but it takes just one person to suck all the gusto out of you.

In ministry this is even truer. You pour your heart out to people and give them all you have, only to find them turn their backs on you.

It is discouraging. More than once you will swear to "never pour out again." Each rejection that you face erodes the love in your heart.

You become cynical and before you know it. You feel no life inside of you.

Very soon, just like those lovely floors of ours, you start to see cracks and holes in your foundation. The teachings and principles that you held so strongly to before start to erode.

You wonder if you heard the Lord correctly. You begin to doubt your call. You look at believers with new eyes. No longer do you desire to give them what they need.

You water down your words. You make it more appealing and simply give the people what they want to keep them happy.

Slowly what was buffed up and shiny becomes dull and lifeless. What went wrong? You lost your sealant! You lost the love that called and released you into His work.

It's time to fill up the holes and get back to the basics of His love once again.

2. BECOMING TOO BUSY

The "busy factor" is a sneaky but deadly corrosive ingredient when it comes to your spiritual life.

You get so busy serving the Lord that you forget to take time to fill up again.

You give out and give out and in the end you convince yourself that you deserve the reward because you are doing "His work."

However, somewhere between receiving that genuine call and fulfilling it, you added a whole lot more of yourself that God never intended.

The work of God becomes difficult and you start to wonder what exactly Jesus said, when he told His disciples,

Matthew 11:30 For My yoke is easy and My burden is light.

You do not find it easy at all. You spend your days having to push doors open and knock walls over.

You face opposition after opposition and you even trick yourself into thinking that this is the way that it should be.

The greatest direction the Lord ever gave me, was the day He told me that He would open the doors. He said that all I needed to do, was to walk through the doors that He opened.

He reminded me that He did not set before me a closed door, but an open one.

My job was to recognize those doors and to walk through them. Simple.

So why have you made it so complicated? Face the reality here. It is not the Lord that is driving you into the ground. It is your own busyness that is doing that.

When you do things God's way, you will accomplish a lot and you will do it in rest.

God calls you to do what He is capable of. It's time to rethink, because you are starting to undo the good foundation that God has laid in your heart.

3. PRESSURE FROM THE WORLD

This is a nasty force that can wipe your feet right from under you. You are walking along doing the work of God and you get side-swiped without warning.

From physical attack to financial attack, you find yourself surrounded. You know that the Lord has called you and that the road that you are on is correct, but the enemy keeps distracting you.

Before you know it, instead of doing the work of the Lord you are running around putting out fires.

You end up taking care of all the natural needs and cares that you forget to take care of your spiritual foundation.

Before you know it, you are worn down and your cracks are showing. You feel like the principles that you learned do not work.

You feel as if the Lord just left you and that you are carrying a mountain of care on your back.

You have fallen prey to the enemy and he has stolen your love and joy! It is time to change tactics.

When you are so busy putting out fires that you can no longer do the things that really count, it is a good sign that the enemy is eroding your sealant.

It is time to do some handiwork once again.

4. YOUR OWN NEED

The age old pity-party is the one sure fire way to strip clean your foundation in five seconds flat. The reason for that is because the love of the Lord is always an outward flow.

The moment you start looking at meeting your own needs in others, you reverse that love in one easy step.

This one follows directly after getting too busy and not taking time with the Lord. As a leader you will always have a lot to do, but the greatest mistake that you can make, is thinking that you have to do all of that work without the Lord.

Suddenly your own needs will rise up. You begin to feel a deep hunger inside. You want others to notice you. You want others to recognize you.

Instead of getting this need met in the Lord, you start to look to your spouse and to those around you.

When they do not meet that need, you become angry and bitter. Now, not only have you eroded the love that you did have, but you begin to strip your foundation so quickly that soon you feel barren and empty.

In place of love, you have bitterness. Instead of hope, you feel depressed. Instead of faith, you feel as if the Lord has abandoned you.

STOP! It's time to retrace your steps and to recover fast. Have your five-minute pity party if you must, but right afterwards, get back on track.

The enemy would be happy to leave you in your cycle of "woe is me."

Here are some good signs that indicate your needs are raging out of control: (Tick off the ones that apply to you right now.)

- o You feel as if no one notices what you do.
- o You just wish everyone would appreciate you for a change.
- o You are angry because you did something special for someone and they did not repay you properly.
- o You feel yourself drawn to those that compliment you or listen to you.

- You find yourself ignoring and overlooking those that just take and do not want to give anything back to you.
- You keep getting into conflicts with your spouse because "they do not understand you" or "are not there for you."
- You feel like a victim that is always picked on.

Can you identify? If so, then your love sealant is way gone! It's time to get patched up.

QUESTIONS FOR REVIEW

1. **What does spiritual wisdom produce?**

   _____

   _____

   _____

2. **What does intuition produce?**

   _____

   _____

   _____

3. **What does communion produce?**

   _____

   _____

   _____

PRACTICAL PROJECT

You gave yourself a quick test in the exercise to see what area you were the weakest in. Now that you have an idea where to start, here are some ways to help get your faith, hope and love in gear!

FAITH:

There is only one way to increase your faith: **Romans 10:17** So then faith [comes] by hearing, and hearing by the [rhema] word of God. It is vital that you meditate on the Word and allow it to sink deep into you. If your faith is week, then take these scriptures and memorize them.

- *Mark 11:23 - For assuredly, I say to you, whoever says to this mountain, 'Be removed and be cast into the sea,' and does not doubt in his heart, but believes that those things he says will be done, he will have whatever he says.*

- *Mark 11:24 - Therefore I say to you, whatever things you ask when you pray, believe that you receive them, and you will have them.*

- *Romans 10:9 - That if you confess with your mouth the Lord Jesus and believe in your heart that God has raised Him from the dead, you will be saved.*

- *Hebrews 11:6 - But without faith it is impossible to please Him, for he who comes to God must believe that He is, and that He is a rewarder of those who diligently seek Him.*

HOPE:

You need a positive picture for the future! But how do you "work up" positive pictures when everything seems so hopeless? Well let us begin with the desires of your heart. What do you desire to do for the Lord? Would you like to flow in the gifts? Would you like to minister? Whatever your desire, as long as it lines up with the Word, is available to you through the Lord!

So to build your hope this is what you are going to do:

1. Make a list of your inner desires. Whether they are for ministry or your personal life.

2. Now write down each one as though it has already been accomplished. In other words, if you desire to have visions write: I am able to see visions. If you desire to see your financial situation come right, then write: My financial situation is in order. My needs are provided.

3. As you do this, pictures will begin to come to your mind. If you desire to minister, you will see an image of yourself ministering.

4. It is important that you do not only SAY the words but also SEE them! You must see the circumstances come right and come in line with your desire.

5. Always be sure to back up your desires with the Word. If you are unsure that your desire is in accordance with the Word, ask your local pastor or mentor to help you out with some scriptures.

As you continue to see the changed image, it will become a reality to you. When your circumstances look bad, you will have those pictures to hold on to and to help you push through!

YOUR INNER DESIRES:
_____
_____
_____
_____
_____
_____
_____
_____
_____
_____
_____

LOVE:

It is not easy to "work up" feelings of love when you are faced with someone that is not very lovable! Yet the Lord commands us to love. Love is not a feeling. It is an act of your will. If you would choose to love and choose to obey the Lord, He will give you what you need to love even the most unlovely person.

Firstly, there is only one true source of love and that is the Lord Jesus. You will find agape love in Him alone. You cannot force love out of your will. You can make a decision to love, but to actually act on that love is not something that comes naturally to us. So you will learn how to love on your knees before the Lord first.

You need to seek a personal relationship with the Lord Jesus. To know Him in an intimate way. It begins with desire. If you desire to know Him and to receive a revelation of who He is, He will answer your prayer. He will reach down and touch you. Did He not do this on the day you got saved?

- Touch the Lord right now where you are. Just a simple prayer from your heart: "Lord I really need to know you in a more intimate way. I want to know who you really are. I want to feel your heart. Oh Lord I so desire to see your face and know your touch. I want to know you like a friend and hear you more clearly than any other person. Reveal yourself to me Lord."

- Now take some time daily to spend in His presence. Either worship, or just talk to Him as if He were standing right next to you.

- As often as you remember, take the time to speak to the Lord. Include Him in your daily tasks. If you are washing dishes, then talk to Him while you are busy. If you are driving your car, then speak to Him about the day ahead.

- The important thing is to bring the Lord to your mind as often as possible.

As you do this you will become very familiar with His gentle presence, and before you know it, a deep relationship would have begun to develop between the two of you. Pouring that love out to others will be an easy next step!

EXERCISE

What are you lacking in your life right now: faith, hope, or love? Each of these is available to you through Christ. As you look to Him now, He is able to give you faith, hope, and love to do the work He has called you to! So check these three levels right now and see where you need work!

Tick off the points that apply to your life right now and see how you score!

FAITH

	After you have prayed, you doubt that the Lord will answer your prayer.
	You are not sure if your faith is strong enough to receive the answers to your prayer.
	You often sit and worry concerning things of the future. You worry about the kids at school, your spouse, what the future holds and how your current circumstances will turn out.
	You know that God is able to provide your needs and desires, but you do not know if He will provide them for YOU.
	Just to play on the safe side, you have insured all valuables, installed alarm systems and put everything you own under lock and key.

HOPE

	If someone had to ask you, "Where do you see yourself two years from now?" you could not give them a clear answer.
	You do not have any short-term goals that go beyond your daily needs and responsibilities, such as the future of the children, what's for dinner and the upcoming vacation.
	You do not see yourself rising up in either the world or ministry, but rather see yourself as carrying on the way you have been going on until now.
	You cannot see yourself being successful in either the world or ministry. You do not see yourself functioning in the gifts like you see others functioning in them.

LOVE

	You struggle to hold your tongue and often find yourself saying things that you knew you should not have said.
	You often misjudge people and those you think are wonderful turn out to be "not so wonderful" while those you judged negatively, turned out to be gems.
	You find it difficult to come to the Lord in prayer and to see Him as a friend and father.
	No matter how hard you try, you find yourself losing your patience with your family, friends, and work colleagues.
	People have often accused you for being harsh or for not understanding them.

If you selected more than 2 points in any of those categories, then you have an idea of where you need to begin working! Perhaps you are weaker on one than on the others, or perhaps all three need work. Whatever your condition the *Practical Project* in this lesson will lead you to strengthen your faith, hope, and love!

EXTRA NOTES

_____

_____

_____

_____

_____

_____

_____

Lesson 08 – Receiving Visions

Based on: *The Way of Dreams and Visions*, Chapter 8

Here is the biggest mistake you can make:

Thinking that you can change the world.

There are those that will receive from us and will change. Even Jesus was clear on this.

> *John 6:37 All that the Father gives Me will come to Me, and the one who comes to Me I will by no means cast out.*

Those that came to Him, Jesus worked with and He saved. Those that did not come and receive from Him, He left to their own devices. He answered the questions of the Pharisees and He certainly put them in their place when they pushed it.

However, He did not go out of His way to try and save them! He said Himself that He was sent to those that were sick and needed a doctor.

Only if someone admits to being sick, can you begin your work.

HOW TO OVERCOME

1. DEALING WITH PEOPLE

So the key here? Work with those that the Lord has really sent to you. Give your heart and love to those that are willing to pay the price.

Jesus was tough! His disciples had to give up all for Him. He even tells us to carry our cross and to follow Him.

He was clear on what He expected from those that followed Him and you must be too. When God sends you someone, you keep on giving until He tells you to stop.

WHAT HAPPENS IF THEY FAIL?

That is not your care is it? When God sends them to you, it is the Lord that you are working for, not them. Do your job. Give as unto the Lord.

Then pray that what you have invested bears fruit. Whether they take what you have is up to them.

If you can see that the work you do is for the Lord, it will change your entire perspective. It will set you free and you will be able to let people go once again.

So who are you working with right now? Ask yourself these questions:

1. Did the Lord send this person to me?

2. Is this person committed to the Lord and to change?

3. Is this person committed to me to receive what I have to give?

4. What instruction has God given me about this person? (Journal to find out God's will for this person.)

Finally, it is only the Lord that can give you the love that you need for others. You will find that love in His presence. Forgive and let the hurts go. Very soon, you will be buffed up and ready to go again!

2. PUTTING "BUSY" BEHIND YOU

If you have found yourself in the "busy trap" then I have only one word for you:

STOP!

It is simple really. Stop it! Right where you are - in the middle of what you are doing. Put the tools down and get into His presence fast.

Sometimes that is all it takes. Close your computer and disconnect the phone. Find those few minutes alone with the Lord.

Take time to journal again and to hear from Him daily. Do not start your day without getting clear direction.

It is a simple matter of walking in the Spirit. Take time to develop that intimate relationship with Jesus again. You have let it go for so long, that you might find it a little difficult at first.

However, do not pick those tools up again or work again until you are secure in Him.

3. OVERCOMING THE WORLD

Ready to kick some serious butt? (Yeah I know... I used a risqué word in a Christian book. Glad to see you are paying attention...)

Well that is the only solution for dealing with the world – to fight! Now I have some incredible news for you.

Check this out:

> *John 16:33 These things I have spoken to you, that in Me you may have peace. In the world you will have tribulation; but be of good cheer, I have overcome the world.*

You see, the enemy would love to trick you into thinking that he has the upper hand, but it takes just a quick reminder to put him back into place again.

When the world is coming against you, it is time that you pick up your weapons of warfare so that you can get back on track again.

Instead of running around putting out fires, take your stand. Pick up the sword of the spirit and stand in faith. You do not need to keep getting beat down.

Deal with the enemy and get it over with, so that you can get back to what really counts.

Often all it takes is a conviction on your part. When you begin to realize that what you are facing is not of the Lord, you have what it takes to overcome.

You do not need to submit to this attack. It is time that you get on the offensive instead of cowering in the corner now.

Bind the works of the enemy and then turn your attention back to what really counts.

Sometimes all it needs is a quick wake up call. Once you get on track again, you will begin to feel the life flowing into your spirit.

The faith, hope, and love will start to increase once again. Often overcoming the greatest blockages is simply getting them out of the way.

The life is already there - all you need to do is remove those big rocks that are preventing the life from flowing out.

4. YOUR NEEDS? NO PROBLEM!

There is only one way to get your needs met and that is to put your running shoes on and sprint into His presence.

I think the problem is that too many folks get so super spiritual when they come into the Lord's presence. Have you ever just taken the time to tell him what is really bothering you?

Sometimes that alone brings peace to your heart. Are you facing a conflict with someone right now?

Are you struggling with a situation right now? Why not tell the Lord about it?

Go and tell Him your problems and concerns. Let it all hang out. Complain to Him if you have to. You can tattle tale, spew and say it like it is.

Once you are done though, take time to listen for His voice in return. Just talking and not listening in any conversation is just plain rude and one-sided.

Perhaps the reason your needs are so exposed right now, is because you have not taken time to listen.

By hearing His voice, you will feel your spirit filling up. You will feel as if the Lord is filling up all those holes in your foundation.

The more you spend time in His presence like that, your heart will be sealed and solid. It will be a foundation that can take a beating.

Not only that, but you will be so filled that you will have more than enough to pour out to others again and again.

WHAT STATE ARE YOU IN?

If you are a minister, then the Lord has called you to be a vessel. That means He will fill you up and pour you out again and again.

So it is safe to assume that your foundation is going to see some heavy traffic.

What kind of condition is your foundation in right now? Is it gleaming with His love, or are you showing signs of wear and tear?

You know what you need and now you also know what to do about it. Get going then and do some handiwork. There is an entire church that needs building and it begins with your foundation.

QUESTIONS FOR REVIEW

1. **What are the two ways in which you can increase your ability to receive visions?**

   _____

   _____

   _____

2. **In which two ways can you release from your spirit to increase the flow of revelation?**

   _____

   _____

   _____

   _____

3. **Can you relive your salvation experience every day?**

   _____

   _____

   _____

4. **Would you like to relive your salvation experience everyday? You can! Reach out now and take it from the Lord's hand.**

PRACTICAL PROJECT: SPEAKING IN TONGUES

When I shared with you on how to receive a vision, I mentioned how powerful it was to use tongues to break through in the Spirit. Well your project for today is to speak for an hour in tongues.

- Find a quiet place and begin speaking in tongues.
- You may not be able to go the full hour the first time – in fact the first 15 minutes are likely to feel like 3 hours! But persevere, working your way up to the full hour.
- If you do not speak in tongues, then this would be a good time to reach out and receive it from the Lord. If you can see visions and journal, you can speak in tongues! It will open an entirely new dimension of the spirit to you and usher you into some glorious times with the Lord Jesus!

EXERCISE

Below is an example of a vision. It is simple and clear. Visions are usually short and to the point. Some people do not even see in full color, receiving a quick flash in their minds. Some people receive an impression in their spirits rather than a complete vision. Wherever you are at right now, you are able to receive visions from the Lord.

"Today I was just talking to the Lord and holding His hand. Then I saw Him on a beautiful horse. He is just incredible. Then I heard the noise like when a sickle is cutting the hay, and I saw a man bent over doing this. He was vigorously gathering tufts of hay and putting them up in a truck. The man turned His head and looked at me smiling, and it was HIM! Then He put a sickle in my hand, and we hugged. Then we both turned and saw a huge field of hay."

IDENTIFY IT!

Read through the vision, then answer the following questions:

   a. **Discern what you feel in the Spirit. How does this vision make you feel?**

   _____
   _____
   _____
   _____

b. Identify the characters and symbols in the vision.

_____
_____
_____
_____
_____
_____
_____

c. What do the characters and symbols represent? (Do not forget to look to the Word for the answers to the symbols).

_____
_____
_____
_____
_____
_____
_____

INTERPRET IT!

Now put these thoughts together and write down what you feel this vision means and compare it to my interpretation at the back of the book.

_____

_____

_____

_____

_____

_____

_____

_____

_____

GROUP PROJECT: THE SECRET PLACE

Take time this week with your group to get into the presence of the Lord Jesus and to bare your innermost fears and thoughts to Him.

There are often questions in our lives that we do not ask the Lord, simply because we are afraid of the answers. It is for you as a trainer to lead your group to the place where they will let down their guard and let God into the places they have been afraid to reveal.

1. **Ask your group to think about any thoughts or conflicts in their life that they have not asked the Lord about.**

Do not be surprised if they have to think long and hard about this question. Often you think that you are not afraid to go to God, but then when He starts digging, you find that there are deep personal things that you have not taken to Him.

Here are some examples that you can use to try and jolt some thoughts in the group.

   a. Conflicts or struggles in their marriage
   b. If God wants them to be married or not
   c. Sexual problems
   d. Financial mistakes
   e. Handling a rebellious child
   f. Submission to a husband
   g. How to love or deal with a wife
   h. How to handle a boss or authority figure
   i. Whether to move to a specific church or city

You would think that people would go to the Lord with these obvious things, but often they think that they must deal with them alone!

2. **Now as everyone thinks about some things that they have not brought to the Lord, allow them to bring it to the Lord right now in prayer and to hold it up to Him.**

If everyone is not afraid to pray openly in front of the group, you can allow the others to share any impressions or visions that they receive regarding this situation.

Keep in mind though that there might be some that might not want to pray out loud because of the intimacy of their question. If this is the case, offer to pray with them privately or to at least journal about it when they get home and to ask the Lord then.

EXTRA NOTES

_____

_____

_____

_____

_____

_____

Part 03

Nightmares, Deception and Demonic Dreams

PART 03 - NIGHTMARES, DECEPTION AND DEMONIC DREAMS

KEY PRINCIPLE

You are not a victim. Because you are in Christ, you can overcome any demonic work in your life.

LESSON 09 - NIGHTMARES, DECEPTION AND DEMONIC DREAMS

Based on: *The Way of Dreams and Visions*, Chapter 9

To assist you in this lesson, I have provided the interpretation for the symbol "Snakes" from *The Way of Dreams and Visions Symbol Dictionary*. The more you flow in visions, the more you are likely to come across demons and snakes. You need not fear the subject of deception, but as you are willing to take a look at it, you guard yourself against it.

It is foolish to think that you will never get into deception. It is also foolish to fear it! We all miss it! You get overwhelmed with daily cares and with the voices of everyone around you. If you ever "miss it" you join the ranks of every other believer who has entered the spiritual realm!

The greater sin is to refuse to learn from your mistakes! Getting into deception or "adding to" a revelation is a human failure. To refuse to look at your sin and failure is a detrimental mistake. This will lead you down a road where the enemy will order your steps.

It is only when you bring your sin and failure into the light that the Holy Spirit is given license into your life once again. So face deception head on!

BE OPEN TO LEARN

Dare you admit that perhaps all of your revelations were not 100% from the Lord? Remember how you learned how revelation has to come through your soul? Well it is not uncommon for your mind to be filled with preconceived ideas. It is common to end a day feeling weary and frustrated.

These little influences have a nasty habit of imposing themselves on the revelation God is giving you. It is only when you are willing to admit this, that the Lord can use you to a greater degree.

If you cannot be open to learn and embrace the concept that you might "miss it" how can the Lord trust you to listen carefully?

If you are so convinced that you are perfect, what more does the Lord have to add to you? Rather err on the side of questioning your revelations and weighing them against the word, than being so dogmatic that you force everyone around you to comply to your ideas and revelations.

Trust me when I say… a little bit of humility goes a long way! Now I do not mean be insecure about what God has told you. By all means, be confident in what you know is God. What I am saying is do not be so prideful that you think every single one of your revelations is fool proof.

The moment you begin thinking like that, I promise that a nice little spiritual lesson is on the way to cut you down to size a bit! The Lord will not have His glory taken!

THIS IS GOD'S REVELATION

At the end of the day, this is the Lord's vision. It is His word and it is His power. You are just a vessel. You do not receive visions and dreams to use them to prove your spirituality to others. Rather it is to stand in humility before others.

The more God uses me, the more His grace humbles me. The more He teaches me and opens my eyes to see the realm of the Spirit, the more I am drawn into His loving arms. The more I want to draw His people into His arms also.

This is the motivation for all revelation – to draw a very cold and weary Church to the passionate and healing arms of Jesus.

THE WAY OF DREAMS AND VISIONS SYMBOL DICTIONARY

SNAKES

The deceptive work of the enemy. Subtle and undetected until its influence is already in full swing.

Positive: The Lord turning the work of the enemy around for our good

Negative:

- Deception
- Subversive attack
- Deliberate sin
- Subtle words repeated in your ear, until you think the thoughts are your own

POSITIVE

I was hard pressed to find a positive representation of a snake in the Word. However, I did manage to find one of interest.

> *Numbers 21:9 So Moses made a bronze **serpent**, and put it on a pole; and so it was, if a serpent had bitten anyone, when he looked at the bronze serpent, he lived*

This symbol of course is used widely in the medical industry (a snake wrapped around a pole). It speaks of the Lord turning everything around for good! Even though the Israelites sinned, He used their very sin to bring them healing.

The serpent on the pole was a representation of what Christ did for us. The serpents in this part of scripture speak of sin. However, Christ became sin for us. Hence the serpent on the pole.

The only time a snake would represent something positive is if it is your trade or you have a pet snake that you care for. If you are a snake removal expert, then it would represent an aspect of your work. Perhaps something that is important to you or representative of your financial income.

NEGATIVE

Snakes never have a positive connotation in dreams and visions. In my personal experience and in looking at the Word, a snake speaks of deception.

The bronze serpent I spoke about previously, while meant for healing turned into an idol that later had to be destroyed by King Hezekiah (2 Kings 18:4)

In personal ministry, I have often seen a serpent wound around the head of a person, speaking lies into their ears. I expose it and tell it to leave.

It also allows me to minister effectively, because then I can encourage the person. I can tell them that the enemy has been lying to them, and that they do not have to listen to his lies any longer!

I have seen various kinds of snakes in the spirit.

I have seen small snakes, which are more of a hindrance than anything serious. They usually come in through association and by reading materials that contain a curse.

Depending on the size of the snake in my dream or vision, it depends on the strength of the demon.

I remember once stumbling on to a website that concentrated on interpreting Scripture into present day experiences. They had taken the Word and had broken it down according to the current events and events of history.

The site seemed innocent enough, even though I did feel a bit of oppression on it.

Soon thereafter everything seemed to go wrong in my life. I felt as if a heavy cloud had come on my head. I found myself getting into conflict with my family, and everything I touched seemed to break!

When I asked for prayer, we saw a serpent attacking me. As I had browsed that site, I had opened my heart to the articles there and actually invited a curse into my life!

I had received a spirit of deception, but as I repented and closed that door, I told the enemy to loose his hold, and the dark cloud around my head lifted immediately!

Cobra/violent snake/viper: Usually when I see a snake like this in the spirit, it speaks of an attack that is not only motivated by deception, but it is also vicious. Vicious words are being spoken against you from someone in deception.

To see a viper, or other such snakes, confirms what Jesus said in this passage.

> *Matthew 12:34 Brood of **vipers**! How can you, being evil, speak good things? For out of the abundance of the heart the mouth speaks*

Python: There was another time in our ministry where I kept seeing a python in the spirit. Others associated with us saw the same thing, and although we knew a snake represented deception, we needed clarification.

It was then that we found out that there was actually a "spirit of python" in the Word. When we looked it up, that specific passage referred to divination. It was very apt to what was going on in the ministry at that time, because the enemy had sent many false prophets to bring strife and conflict.

As we came against that spirit, those operating in the spirit of divination suddenly left, and things immediately calmed down again.

It is interesting that God had Moses and Aaron use serpents against Pharaoh's magicians who operated in witchcraft and divination. The message? God is greater than your spirit of divination!

Here is the reference to the "spirit of python" in the Greek and the corresponding passage:

4436 Puthon {poo'-thone}

from Putho (the name of the region where Delphi, the seat of the famous oracle, was located); TDNT - 6:917,*; n m

AV - divination 1; 1

1) in Greek mythology the name of the Pythian serpent or dragon that dwelt in the region of Pytho at the foot of Parnassus in Phocis, and was said to have guarded the oracle at Delphi and been slain by Apollo

2) a spirit of divination

> Acts 16:16 Now it happened, as we went to prayer, that a certain slave girl possessed with a **spirit of divination** met us, who brought her masters much profit by fortune:

Lies and deception:

> Genesis 3:13 And the Lord God said to the woman, What is this you have done? The woman said, **The serpent deceived me**, and I ate.

QUESTIONS FOR REVIEW

1. **What are the three ways in which a person can be deceived?**

   _____

   _____

   _____

2. **How do you identify a spirit of divination?**

   _____

   _____

   _____

3. How does divination differ from false revelation?

4. What is the most common mistake a person makes when misinterpreting their dreams or visions?

PRACTICAL PROJECT: PREVENTING DECEPTION

The best way to prevent deception in your own life is to identify how the Lord would speak to you, how your own mind sounds and how the enemy sounds. Unfortunately, though these are lessons that we all learn the hard way! In training the prophets, many have come to me and said, "Oh why did I have to fall into deception! Why do I have to face this?" I answer that question the same way every time and that is with, "Unless you know what the voice of the enemy sounds like, you will never learn how to avoid it!"

So if you have fallen into deception yourself, do not feel like a second rate Christian! Use what the enemy has tried on you and turn it for the Lord's glory! Use his very deception against him. Below is a table that I want you to keep for a week. As you go to prayer and receive visions, dreams, or any other kind of revelation from the Lord, write down how you felt at the time of receiving the revelation and write also how the revelation was received.

It would be a good idea to check all revelation through the "Deception Checklist" before proceeding here.

REVELATION:	DATE:

Emotion:

How you received it:

REVELATION:	DATE:

Emotion:

How you received it:

REVELATION:	**DATE:**

Emotion:

How you received it:

REVELATION:	**DATE:**

Emotion:

How you received it:

ASSESS THEM!

Now that you have received and written down your revelations, read the points below and confirm that they were from the Lord. You should be able to identify at least one point from the emotions and one from the listening categories for every revelation you received.

EMOTIONS:

a. You were convicted and motivated to action.
b. You felt a deep sense of love and adoration towards the Lord or particular people He brought to your mind.
c. You came to the Lord feeling discouraged and depressed, but left feeling encouraged and motivated.
d. You arrived confused, but left at peace.
e. You came with a list of problems and frustrations, but left feeling at peace and in control again.
f. You went into prayer and a Godly anger came over you – you may have ended up interceding on behalf of another and speaking blessing or release over them.
g. You felt a sense of awe and a deep respect for the Lord.
h. Your emotions were stirred and you were motivated into praise and worship.
i. You felt a deep grief within and travailed on behalf of another – this would also fall into the category of intercession.

LISTENING / HOW YOU RECEIVED IT:

a. You received your revelation very quietly. Perhaps a feeling within that began softly and grew. A gentle nudging in a certain direction through a dream or vision. If you heard an inner voice, it was quiet and gentle. If you saw a vision, the vision came back to you repeatedly and gently.

This is how the Holy Spirit will speak to you.

b. The revelation was very clear. It came unexpectedly and was very logical. When you received the revelation, you were not surprised by it, because it was in line with what you had been feeling all along. For example: You had been feeling that it was time that your church or pastor moved in a certain direction and in prayer you received a word confirming this very clearly.

This is the voice of your own mind. It is very seldom that the Lord will say what you expect Him to say... that is why when we really do hear from Him, it is called REVELATION!

c. You received your revelation very clearly. It was loud and in tremendous detail. The inner voice was VERY clear and loud almost. You could almost hear it above the noises around you. The revelation took you by surprise, because you were not thinking along those lines at that time. You were going about your own daily business when a revelation suddenly came into your mind with complete clarity.

Be very careful! This is how the enemy speaks! He is convincing, stirs your emotions and pushes you beyond what God intended. Even something that might seem good to do, when done in access is devastating!

EXERCISE: DECEPTION CHECK LIST!

No matter what revelation you receive or what revelation others give you to interpret, before going anywhere you must check their revelation against the following points. If the revelation even has one of these points, proceed with caution and further check the revelation against the Word.

- 1. The person felt fear when they received the revelation.

- 2. When the revelation was shared, the person receiving was made to fear.

- 3. The revelation condemned and accused, thus causing the person in question to feel depressed. This kind of condemnation is NOT conviction as it does not motivate the person to action, but rather makes them withdraw and regress. (Brings death)

- 4. The revelation was pushy - demanding that action was taken immediately!

- 5. The revelation overrode a person's will. Anything they do not have control of is not of the Lord as the Holy Spirit is a dove and does not override the will of man.

- 6. The revelation was received through very loud words. A strong voice, a strong forceful vision or dream.

- 7. Anything that veils its identity is not of God. If an angelic being appears, not showing its face and pushing the person to receive from it, then it is not of God. The Lord and His angels are always open-faced. If such a being appears, it is an angel of light and should be told to leave in the name of Jesus.

- 8. A revelation that brings confusion and doubt is not of the Lord. If a person is thrown into turmoil, once again regressing and not motivated to positive action, then the revelation was not of the Lord or perhaps even shared in the wrong season.

Sometimes we have just accepted certain symbols to mean certain things – but take NOTHING for granted if the revelation is not based on the Word! Check every single symbol and direction with the Word of God and see if it lines up. I recommend a good Bible concordance. If you can get one on CD for your computer, even better, because you can then look up scriptures all having the same symbols.

Above all else discern the spirit on the revelation by the gift of discerning of spirits. If you get a knot in your stomach, feel uneasy or simply feel a "no no" in the Spirit, then proceed with caution. However, if you feel comfortable, positively motivated and a "yes yes" in the Spirit then the Word is of the Lord.

EXTRA NOTES

_____

_____

_____

_____

_____

_____

_____

LESSON 10 - THE SIGNS OF DECEPTION

Based on: *The Way of Dreams and Visions*, Chapter 10

I would daresay that the greatest open door to deception lies in a single word: pride!

It is a dangerous place when you need to get a revelation to prove your standing with God. It is a fateful day when you stand up to declare a word to bolster your own name among the nations.

As you have already learned in *The Way of Dreams and Visions*, deception comes because of a number of reasons. Let me add to that a little bit over here.

HOW DECEPTION ENTERS

1. IMPARTATION

When you receive a spiritual impartation from someone who is bound by deception. I cover this extensively in *Prophetic Warrior*, so I will not labor the point here.

2. DOCTRINE

When you conform your mind to the ideas of man and the enemy, this gives root to deception. Instead of having the mind of Christ, you have the mind of the world and are influenced by the enemy. Heretical doctrine is one of the greatest anchors for a spirit of divination and deception. The reason being that it is more than just a demonic bondage – but a concrete way of thought that continues to breed demonic influence.

3. GENERATIONAL BONDAGES

It is common to have continued demonic influence from your family, especially when you received a lot from them. Having worked with prophets for many years, I have seen many who received a spirit of divination or deception from their parents. Having grown up with that influence their entire lives, as they enter into the spiritual realm for themselves, they take the spirit of deception on as their own.

4. DABBLING IN THE SPIRIT REALM

If you enter the realm of the spirit without the blood of Christ, you are signing up for trouble! You will find yourself in the battlefield of the enemy unarmed. This is exactly what happens when you dabble in witchcraft, false religion, tarot card reading, New Age and anything else that encourages spiritual experiences outside of Christ.

5. SEXUAL RELATIONS

When we have sexual intercourse, it runs a lot deeper than a physical connection. As a result, when you sleep with someone, you receive what is in their spirit also. This holds true for abuse, molestation and casual sex. I cover this in Chapter 9 of *Prophetic Warrior*, if you want to read more up on that.

6. PRIDE

Of all the doors that deception finds its way through, pride is the largest. When you are afraid of what people think of you, you will seek for revelation on demand.

When you are insecure and you desperately want to be recognized, your revelations find you the acclaim you so desperately need.

When you have faced so much rejection and you just need a word to prove your case, you breed a ground that is ripe for the enemy to sow seed into!

Pride comes in many forms, however in each case, the message is the same, "But what about me!"

The revelation no longer becomes a tool for ministry, but one to meet your own need. I do not think that any of us would like to think that we revel in the accolades of others when they hear our visions, but dare you be honest with yourself? If you were, you would realize that it effects you when people rave about your visions. It effects you when people reject your revelations.

It is not the feeling that is sin... it is what you do what it afterwards. It is when you begin to dig deeper and go further and hunger for greater experiences to meet that inner need that will lead you to a place you should not go to.

THE SECRET WEAPON: GET REAL!

Want to walk on the narrow road? Its simple – get real! Get in touch with your hurts and what you feel within. Get in touch with your strong emotions about a person and a topic and ask yourself, "Is this word of God, or is it just feeding what I want to hear?"

Test yourself so that the Lord does not have to! If you are willing to test your own heart, you need not fear deception. If you are open to dump any vision or dream at any time, you need not fear deception.

THE WORLD WILL NOT END...

The thing is, the Lord is not about to run out of dreams and visions! He has plenty more to share with you. If you have to let a vision go, relax! He is well able to confirm that word to you through others.

You will not let God down by putting a revelation aside as you wait for confirmation. Once that confirmation comes though, then it is time to act on it and to remain obedient. Most of the time though, we are just too afraid to test our own revelations!

You do not want to imagine that you would miss God. You do not want to think about what the truth would be, if what you are holding on to so dearly, is a lie.

Let it go. Ours is a walk of faith and moments like these are the greatest test of that faith. Let your trust be, not in your revelations, but in the Lord!

THE WAY OF DREAMS AND VISIONS SYMBOL DICTIONARY

DEMONS

It is common to see demons both in dreams and visions. Seeing these beings indicates that you are functioning in the gift of discerning of spirits.

The Lord will reveal these things to you at His bidding, but if you are having demonic manifestations or coming face to face with demonic forces that you cannot control, realize that the enemy has been given license in your life and you need to deal with it accordingly.

CHARACTER SPECIFIC AND UNIVERSAL SYMBOLS

I often see demons in the spirit and I will give you a quick summary here of the different levels of demons. You can then relate this to what you have experienced and seen in the spirit:

> *Ephesians 6:12 For we wrestle not against flesh and blood, but against* **principalities, against powers, against the rulers of the darkness** *of this world, against spiritual wickedness in high [places]. (KJV)*

> *1 Corinthians 2:8 Which none of the princes of this world knew: for had they known it, they would not have crucified the Lord of glory. (KJV)*

The following descriptions have been based on *The Prophetic Warrior*. You will find all the Scripture references and full explanations in this book. The following is simply a summary.

Principality demons: These are usually your spirits of infirmities. I see them in the spirit as insects, small crustaceans and so forth. I remember one time really suffering with a pinched sciatic nerve on my left side. The pain was unbearable, shooting from my hip and down my leg, sometimes even making my leg feel lame.

My husband Craig prayed for me and in the spirit he saw what looked like a scorpion on the nerve pinching it. By identifying the spirit of infirmity, he told it to go and I felt an instant relief. The pain and the condition cleared up and by the next day I was walking around as if nothing had happened.

By identifying the spirit of infirmity when praying for someone and telling it to leave will often bring an immediate result.

What I share here is based on my personal experience. You may see these demons in a different way. This is just a guideline for you to follow and help you identify what you may be seeing.

Power demons: These demons are a little stronger and are what are associated to things like depression, discouragement and deception. (See _Snakes_ for more on deception)

They are what attacks us in our day-to-day walk. These are the demons that are also given the most license through association with others and by contamination through family generations.

We see these demons often like monkeys or gorillas hanging on and attacking.

Ruler demons: These demons are stronger and look a bit more human in the spirit. The ruler demons are occult in nature and if someone is possessed then there is a ruler demon involved. I often see an occult demon as a broad shouldered, strong-looking demon. Sometime green or grey in color with a bald head and pointy ears.

Some people see these spirits as your typical "devil-pointed ears, forked tongue" kind of creature. These demons are given license through personal or generational sin involving, witchcraft, false religion, freemasonry, horoscopes, fortune-telling and so forth.

I have seen the prince of death and he looks like an emaciated black being. Thin and evil. I have seen the prince of lust. He is attractive, almost feminine in appearance and is dressed lavishly in many different colored silks. When I see this demon, I know that the person I am ministering to is bound by lust.

These are just a few, but you should be able to identify for yourself what you are coming against.

Jezebel spirit: I see the Jezebel spirit as a witch who is haggard and aggressive. When ministering to someone and I see this, I know that counseling as well as deliverance will be needed. I have found this particular demon to be quite aggressive – like with any demon, the person in question will need to deal with personal sin before they can break free.

Princes:

> *Ephesians 2:2 In which in time past you walked according to the course of this world, according to the **prince** of the authority of the air, the spirit that now works in the children of disobedience*

These demons coordinate and arrange entire structures to help them fulfill their purpose.

This is where you will find your territorial spirits. You will have princes with varied influences.

To name a few of them: family generational princes, territorial princes, and princes who are in control of specific archetypes.

What separates them from the other categories, is that they build the structure in which the other demons can fulfill their purpose.

Territorial demons: The princes are very human in appearance and can even be "good looking" at times. These are the demons placed over an area such as the prince of Persia mentioned in the Word. Yes, there is a prince of America, Mexico, Africa, and every other country, state, and province of the earth. They are given license through the sin and the words of man.

I have seen the prince of America as a half-bull and half-man. Having the face of a man, but the horns of a bull. We have seen the prince of Mexico as looking like a type of Indian chief, with a full feather headdress on.

Wickedness in high places: There are seven main categories of princes that rule the systems of this world. I teach on them in *The Strategies of War*.

Here I will mention the three main leaders of the demonic realm. The first being Lucifer who is in charge of the religious system. The second is Apollyon who is in charge of the world and the attack on us directly, and Pharaoh, who is in charge of the world system and referred to as "The God of This World."

Lucifer: Usually attractive looking – do not assume the enemy is unattractive! He was after all, the son of the morning.

> *Isaiah 14:12 How you are fallen from heaven, O **Lucifer**, son of the morning! How you are cut down to the ground, you who weakened the nations!*

Apollyon: I usually see him as half-human and half-reptilian in the spirit. Note that demons are disembodied spirits – how you see them might differ from the way the Lord shows them to me.

> *Revelation 9:11 And they had as king over them the angel of the bottomless pit, whose name in Hebrew is Abaddon, but in Greek he has the name **Apollyon**.*

Pharaoh: I usually see him as a pharaoh of old, sitting on a huge throne surrounded by the banks of the world.

> *2 Corinthians 4:4 In whom the **god of this world** hath blinded the minds of them which believe not, lest the light of the glorious gospel of Christ, who is the image of God, should shine unto them.*

Please Note: If you are having encounters with demons that are leading to actual physical experiences, this denotes an open door in your life that is given satan license to attack you! I recommend that you get one of our books or contact one of our staff through any of our websites for counsel as soon as possible to overcome this bondage in your life!

QUESTIONS FOR REVIEW

1. **What are the three signs that a revelation is a deception?**

   _____

   _____

   _____

2. **Why is a person attacked with a demonic dream?**

   _____

   _____

   _____

3. Name two ways in which a door can be opened to a curse in a person's life.

4. What is the main difference between a warning dream and a deceptive dream?

PRACTICAL PROJECT: IDENTIFYING CURSES

1. I want you to think back, can you identify any nightmares you might have had in the past?

_____

_____

_____

_____

2. **Can you remember the events in your life that surrounded that time of the dream?**

_____

_____

_____

_____

3. **It is important that you identify where exactly the enemy had an open door to attack you.**

_____

_____

_____

If you are still struggling with nightmares, then he still has an open door and you need to take a good look at your own life and relationships.

- A good place to start would be to go through your bedroom and see if you have brought anything into it that is contrary to the Word and spirit of the Lord.
- Written materials such as books, magazines, letters or newspapers are a good starting point.

- After that look for any ornaments or objects that you brought around the time your nightmares began.
- If you still cannot find anything, then look to the Lord to reveal any new relationships or even old friends you have struck up a relationship with that are under a curse.
- Above all else ask the Lord for revelation to direct you to where the open door is. We do not want to 'witch hunt' but simply want to find that open door to the enemy and close it in Jesus name!

EXERCISE

EXERCISE 1: IDENTIFYING DECEPTION

After reading or listening to this chapter can you identify anyone (perhaps even yourself) who you think is operating in a spirit of divination?

- Think back on events of the past or stories you were told of people who knew terrible events before they happened.

_____

_____

_____

_____

- Can you remember how you felt when this story was shared?

_____

_____

_____

_____

_____

- Did you feel uncomfortable or perhaps indifferent?

_____

_____

_____

The key here is to identify how you felt at the time of being exposed to any kind of deception. If you can identify how you felt both in your body, emotions, and deep in your spirit, when you feel this again, it will be a sign to you to be wary of what is being shared.

It is up to you to guard your own heart from falsehood and as you identify deception and learn to sense when something is not right in the Spirit, the enemy will not be able to lead you astray.

EXERCISE 2: DISCERNING THE SPIRITS

When you first begin to flow in the gift of discerning of spirit you are likely to sense it in one or more of the following points. Can you identify any of these in your own life?

- A knot in your stomach, sometimes even nausea.

- A deep feeling inside that says "No!"

- Discomfort or a feeling of foreboding.

- The atmosphere of the air suddenly gets thicker, almost like the lights have dimmed (but in reality have not).

- You feel an external pressure bearing down on you. A pushing down.

- You may have physical manifestations like feeling like "your skin is crawling."

- You may have a tingling or a "pulling" sensation in your hands when you come into confrontation with someone who is under a curse or in deception.

- You might smell something amiss. Common smells are sulfur, a rotten smell, or a damp musty smell.

- In vision, you are likely to see the spirit involved in the deception or attack.

GROUP PROJECT

Everyone has nightmares! Sometimes though not all bad dreams are nightmares and it is important that your group learns to identify the difference.

a. Begin your group project by getting each person to share a nightmare with the group.

b. Give the others a chance to help identify if this was indeed a nightmare or simply a negative dream with a clear warning message.

c. Get everyone to identify WHY they feel that this dream was a nightmare.

d. Get the person who had the nightmare to identify the open door in their lives that brought this nightmare on.

EXTRA NOTES

_____

_____

_____

_____

_____

_____

_____

PART 04

INTERPRETING SYMBOLS IN DREAMS AND VISIONS

PART 04 - INTERPRETING SYMBOLS IN DREAMS AND VISIONS

KEY PRINCIPLE

The Spirit of the Lord is not like the wisdom of man. It comes by revelation and it comes supernaturally. This should always be your motivation when interpreting dreams and visions.

LESSON 11 – INTERPRETING SYMBOLS IN DREAMS AND VISIONS

Based on: *The Way of Dreams and Visions*, Chapter 12

I have covered the various interpretations for symbols in *The Way of Dreams and Visions book and Symbol Dictionary*. However, I will lay out a few common symbols for you here.

What I am going to do is get right down to the "brass tacks" of handling symbols by sharing my own examples with you.

So, imagine that we are sitting in my lounge and across the way is someone sharing their dream with me. As they share, I am ministering and as you sit next to me on that couch, I turn to you from time to time and explain to you what I am doing.

POPULAR SYMBOLS

There are so many symbols to interpret that it would take another hundred books to list them all. Instead what I am going to do here is pick out ten of the most popular symbols that I come across all of the time. These symbols are ones that I find coming up in my own dreams or in the dreams of others I minister to.

Jesus used parables to illustrate spiritual principles to the people of his day. He used pictures that were common to them. In the same way the Lord will still use symbols in our dreams that are common to us. The Lord still speaks to us in parables, even in our dreams.

So these symbols are also ones that span across cultures and denominations (Universal Symbols). So by arming yourself with some good knowledge here, you will also start picking up the wisdom you need to minister effectively.

As we work through them together, you will find that you can identify them in your own life. If this happens, fantastic! It means you will be better equipped to minister to others.

1. GIVING BIRTH OR BEING PREGNANT

A baby speaks of something new being born in you. This is not always a positive thing. It can be negative as well. Not all of the things that we conceive in our lives are good. Not everything that you conceive in the Spirit is something that you want. So it is important to discern if the pregnancy or the birth is positive.

If you dream of being pregnant, it means that you have conceived something. Say for example you have been studying a prophetic or teaching course and you dream that you are pregnant. It is a confirmation from the Lord that something has been conceived in you.

The principles that you are learning have started to take root in your spirit. It is a lovely dream telling you that your new ministry has been conceived and will be born.

Example

I remember when I had been released into ministry training, about three months into it I had such a clear dream. I dreamed that I was three months pregnant. I did not realize at the time that I had been on that road three months already.

The Lord was confirming that I was exactly on the track that God wanted me to be on. It was a message to nurture this new ministry and to continue pressing on with it.

That is an important aspect of this kind of dream. In the natural, an expectant mother cannot just eat what she wants to. In the Spirit, it is the same. If you dream of being pregnant, it is not only a confirmation that you have conceived something new in the Spirit, but also a message to nurture and care for that new thing.

People think, "I have been called to ministry. The Lord will take care of the rest." Yes, sure He will take you through the training, but you have to submit to it. A mother does not just let the baby take care of itself. No, she has to care for it. It is up to you to take care of your calling.

FOR THE MEN

Now as a man, you might not dream that you are pregnant. You could dream instead that your wife is pregnant and it would have the same interpretation. Because your wife is one with you, if you dream she is pregnant or giving birth, it means that you are birthing something new.

MISCARRIAGE. LOSING THE BABY

Perhaps you dream that you lose the baby or that it is born dead. At first that sounds like a terrible dream. However, think about it for a bit. Could it be that the thing that you have conceived is not of God? In which case, dreaming of a miscarriage, this is a good dream.

Perhaps you were involved in a relationship in the past and you dream of being pregnant from that person or that time in your life. In your dream, your circumstances take you back to that time in your life. Your dream is indicating that you conceived something back in that time that has now been brought to death.

While that might seem negative but actually it could well be that it is exactly what God wants to do in your life right now. Perhaps he is calling you to let an old vision die or to let go of an old responsibility.

Not everything we conceive in the Spirit is positive. There are times we receive negative things. On the other hand, there are times when season pass and the Lord calls us to pick up new ministries and mandates, meaning you have to let the old go.

GIVING BIRTH/HOLDING A BABY

To dream of giving birth or of holding a baby speaks of a new responsibility that you have been given. Again, this dream has a double meaning.

On the one hand, the Lord has given you a ministry or a calling and placed it into your hands, but on the other, your job just begins! It is for you now to take hold of that calling and to do something with it.

I never saw a baby that was born and left to take care of itself. It is for you to work from there.

Breastfeeding

This is especially true of dreaming of breastfeeding a baby. It means that you are investing everything you are and all of your strengths into this new spiritual baby. When this speaks of your ministry, this is a fantastic picture.

It means that the Lord is confirming that now is the time to put your full effort into this ministry. He is encouraging you to put everything into this one thing instead of running around wasting your time on other things that do not matter.

GIVING BABY AWAY/OTHER PEOPLE'S BABIES.

You can have dreams where you give your baby away. This is a confirmation that the ministry you are working with, it something that the Lord wants you to hand over to someone else. The Lord wants you to hand the care of that ministry over to someone else, so that He can give you something new.

At first, this might seem negative, but if you understand the symbol, it is quite positive. This is not easy of course. The ministry has become your baby and you have put your heart and soul into it and it is not easy to pass it on. However, until you are prepared to do this, you will not receive the new baby that the Lord has for you.

Now there is also a negative side. What if you keep dreaming that you are taking other people's babies or that you keep being handed other people's babies?

Do you know the English expression, "That's not my baby!"

Why do you think we say that? It speaks of our responsibilities and cares. So if you keep being dumped with other people's babies in your dreams, it means that other people keep dumping their junk on you.

They are putting their responsibility on you and instead of investing your time into the ministry God has given to you, you are running around investing into the ministry of others. This is a negative dream.

The Lord is trying to say, "You are so busy running around fussing over everyone else and putting so many fires out, that you are not taking care of the ministries and gifts that I have given to you."

People do not like to hear that interpretation very much. They like to hear that they are a nice person who just runs around helping others with their ministry. However, it is one thing to be a foster parent, it is another to give birth to your own child. Even as a father, you want your own child.

You do not want to always give back the babies you care for. Instead you want to have your own child and see it grow up.

There is an exception however. You might dream that someone gives you their baby for a season that you take care of. Then when that season is over, you hand the baby back. In this case, the Lord is indicating that there is some task that you are going to do, but it is not permanent. You will be there to help these people get off the ground, but you will not stay.

Remember, it is their baby – it is not your baby. This season is temporary.

2. DEATH

A dream like this is also very contradictory. You would think that dreaming of someone dying or of death would be bad, but the opposite is often true.

To dream of death often means that the Lord is bringing and aspect of your flesh to death so that you can resurrect with something new.

Now what about a dream where a person keeps trying to get out of the coffin and will not die? What a horrible dream! Do you know what it means? It means that whatever aspect of yourself that the Lord is trying to crucify in you, keeps coming back to life.

You refuse to die and let go! It is time for you to bury that nasty flesh so that the Lord can be glorified in you. This kind of dream or vision is common to someone going through an intense fivefold ministry training.

You keep dreaming that someone keeps sitting up in a coffin and the Lord is saying to you, "Die already!"

And you respond with, "But Lord I did die! I let it all go."

"If you died, then you would not flinch! A dead body does not sit up!"

When Jesus died, He truly died. He only rose up when the Father revived Him. If you are in prophetic training or office, get ready for this! The Lord will call you to death again and again so that you can become more effective for Him.

Each time that you rise up in your flesh or try to do things your way, you can bet that a good 'death experience' is on the way.

PEOPLE YOU KNOW OR BABIES DYING

Perhaps you dream of a close family member dying. The first thing you need to identify is what that person means to you. That will give you a good indication of what the Lord is trying to bring to death in you.

This is something to keep in mind when you are interpreting for others. You need to ask them what that person means to them in real life.

Now what happens if you dream one of your babies dies? The Lord is saying, "I am taking you through a death of a vision."

If the dream is negative, then one of your ministries or something you are involved with is under attack at the moment and the enemy is trying to destroy it.

3. CRYING IN YOUR SLEEP

Most people have done it. I have even been known to giggle in my sleep from time to time. (No...you are not the only one!) So what is that all about? Rest assured that this is nothing to worry about. This is simply a purging dream.

It means that all the tension that you have built up is being released. Perhaps you dream of something from your past and that causes the crying. This could mean that the Lord is bringing a healing in that area in your life. On the other hand, it could mean that He is exposing an area in your life that still needs healing.

If you suspect that there is an emotional wound that the Lord is exposing, do not be afraid. The Lord is exposing it only to heal it. He is not exposing it to hurt you.

4. YOUR HOUSE

This symbol is as common as the one on babies. It is good to remember that the house you dream about speaks of your life. Now it is not often that you will dream of the actual house your live in right now.

In your dreams, the house might look different to what you have now, but in the dream it is your house. You might even dream of houses you grew up in or have certain memories of. In each case the house belongs to you and so represents an aspect of your own life.

We are the temple of the Holy Spirit and dreaming of a house is a picture of what is happening in you right now.

NEW ROOMS

Say for example that you dream you suddenly discover new rooms in your house. When I first started moving more into the arts I kept having a dream like that and at first I could not understand what it meant. My father interpreted it for me and said that there were some untapped areas in my life that I had never tried going into before.

However, now was the time to tap into that hidden potential. After I received the interpretation, I did not have the dreams any more. The interpretation was clear. I had to go into areas that I always had, but had never developed.

HOUSE BEING TORN DOWN OR RENOVATED

Of course there was the time I dreamed my entire house was being torn down! Bad dream! Do you know what it means? It means that the Lord is about to do some renovating in your life. And you know, it is not a lot of fun to have a wall knocked down. It is not comfortable at all.

So if you dream of something like that, then get ready for some shaking in your life. The Lord is about to change your foundation and give you a face lift. If you are in ministry, then deal with it! Your house is going to be changed more often than you can count.

When someone comes to you for an interpretation of dreams involving their house, you now have an answer for them. It all depends on what is happening in the house. If the house is being expanded, it means that the Lord is going to expand them.

Just by knowing that the house represents your life, the interpretation opens up immediately.

QUESTIONS FOR REVIEW

1. **When is the only time that you will receive the revelation for your symbols in the Word?**

   _____
   _____
   _____

2. **Why is it that the interpretation of symbols differs from person to person?**

   _____
   _____
   _____
   _____

3. What part do morals play in dream interpretation?

_____

_____

_____

_____

4. What part do your fears play in dream interpretation?

_____

_____

_____

_____

_____

_____

PRACTICAL PROJECT: YOUR INTERNAL DREAM

I would like you to document a dream that you feel is an internal dream. View the Dream Category Checklist in the previous lesson to identify an internal dream.

1. **Write the dream out in full.**

_____

_____

_____

2. List all the characters in your dream.

3. List all the objects in your dream. This would include, animals, insects, plants, furnishing, etc.

4. **List all buildings and landscapes in your dream.**

_____

_____

_____

5. **List all the colors in your dream.**

_____

_____

_____

In the next lesson we will begin looking at how to interpret these characters and objects, but for now just break the dream down as I have indicated.

EXERCISE: DREAM CATEGORY CHECKLIST

Below is a checklist for you to use in identifying the category of any dream. With each dream that you receive to interpret, put it past the Deception Checklist FIRST – then once you are confident that the revelation is truly of the Lord, put it through this checklist and identify which category it falls into.

As you do this you will learn to identify all dreams at a simple glance and the Holy Spirit can take it from there.

HEALING DREAM:

If you can see most of these points in the dream, then it is a Healing Dream and is a wonderful sign that the Lord has brought a healing to an area of this person's life.

- Characters in the dream were from the past. Some examples are school days, childhood events, and experiences in adolescence, situations in previous workplaces. Old conflicts with people in authority. Old friends, teachers or family.

- Objects, symbols, houses, landscapes, towns were from memories in the past.
- A victory was achieved in this dream.
- The person woke up from this dream feeling good.
- Perhaps a confrontation took place, but the outcome was positive.
- The dream does not necessarily make complete sense, but a definite positive outcome was the end result.

PURGING/GARBAGE DREAM:

If the dream you have been given has even three of these points, then it is no doubt a Purging/Garbage dream and has no interpretation. It is possible to look into a dream like this and know exactly what has been on the person's mind; their fears, hope and frustrations – because they would have acted them all out in this dream. Unbelievers also have these kinds of dreams.

- The dream is very complicated with many scene changes.
- Emotions run high, from anger, lust, jealousy, joy, laughter...any emotion blown out of proportion.
- The person is usually an active character in the dream.
- There are many symbols, many characters, and many objects in this dream. Too many to mention.
- The dream took a good portion of the night.
- The person could have woken up either refreshed from having expressed all their hidden anger.
- They could also have woken up quite weary from all the fighting and running in their dream.
- This kind of dream sounds like something that should be made into a movie!

INTERNAL DREAM:

If you can identify most of these points in the dream, then the dream is a clear Internal dream. In other words, the dream is a representation of the condition of their spiritual life past and present. It is the condition of their lives RIGHT NOW. Unbelievers also have these kinds of dreams.

- The dream is short and to the point.

- It is often followed or proceeded by other short dreams carrying a similar message.

- The person in question is actively involved in the dream – he is one of the characters.

- All the characters are familiar to the person.

- They might have an unidentified male or female character in their dream representing their masculine and feminine side.

- All the objects and landscapes are something they are familiar with. Things are where they should be. They are objects that they come into contact with often.

- All objects in the dream would not be out of place for the person in question to come across in their every day life.

INTERNAL PROPHETIC DREAM:

This would indicate an internal prophetic dream. This means that all characters and symbols in this dream are a representation of a part the person having the dream. However, this dream is an indication of the condition of their spiritual lives, present and future. It is a message of the Lord for those things that lie ahead. It is a word of wisdom for things to come. Perhaps the Lord would use such a dream to indicate a death to the flesh that is to come or perhaps a promotion in the body of Christ.

These dreams give counsel, direction, motivation and a word from the Lord. You will learn later on how to apply this revelation to the life of the person.

- The dream is short and to the point.

- It is often followed or proceeded by other short dreams carrying a similar message.

- The person in question is actively involved in the dream – he is one of the characters.

- They might have an unidentified male or female character in their dream representing their masculine and feminine side.

- Some of the characters and objects are familiar to the person.

- Some of the objects and characters are unfamiliar.

- While some objects and symbols are things they would come across in every day living, it is mixed in with other objects that they would not ordinarily come across.

EXTERNAL PROPHETIC DREAM:

These are the criteria pointing to an external prophetic dream. This means that the characters can very well be who they are, or could represent a specific type of person or group. For example, a pastor in such a dream could represent ALL pastors universally and not just the individual. A mother could represent the church universally and a president could be the representation of the world's system.

If a person is having dreams like this often, they it is possible that they are called to a prophetic ministry.

- The dream is short and to the point.

- It is often followed or proceeded by other short dreams carrying a similar message.

- The person in question is not actively involved in the dream. He is very likely standing without looking in as if it were a movie being displayed before him.

- The characters can be either familiar or unfamiliar.

- The person cannot seem to fit the interpretation into an internal application.

- The characters, objects and symbols are not portrayed in the same way they usually are in their dreams. For example, if they have identified a certain person in their dreams as a part of themselves - in this dream this representation does just not seem to fit.

- Most of the objects and surroundings are unfamiliar to the person.

EXTRA NOTES

LESSON 12 - INTERPRETING CHARACTERS IN DREAMS AND VISIONS

Based on: *The Way of Dreams and Visions*, Chapter 12

Continuing with our symbols from the previous lesson, take time to identify what your family members mean in your dream!

5. RELATIVES

I have given such a lengthy description of this one in *The Way of Dreams and Visions Symbol Dictionary*, but let me just say that you will dream of relatives and close friends very often.

Now is the time to be honest and consider what you really think of that person. And so the easiest way to assess what a relative means in your dream is to do this:

1. Close your eyes and say their name.

2. What is the first word that comes to your mind?

What is the first image or impression that comes to your mind? How about we apply this now and play a little game together.

I am going to write down a list of a few people that should be fairly common to your life. After you read each one on the list, close your eyes, say their name and then write down the first word or impression that comes to you.

If nothing comes to your mind as you go through the list, do not worry! It could be that they are not a common symbol in your life. This is just a practice round and one that you can use with others as you minister.

Here goes!

1. Mother

2. Father

3. Mother In-Law

4. Father In-Law

5. Eldest Sister

6. Your Eldest Child (If you have children)

7. Husband/Wife

When I dream of my husband, I know the Lord is speaking of my relationship with Jesus. When I dream of my relationship with my husband, I know that Jesus is pointing out areas that I need to work on or perhaps good things that He is doing.

My father though, is a picture of God the Father in my dreams and these dreams speak of my direction for ministry. Just as our Heavenly Father opens doors for us or closes them.

STRUGGLING WITH INTIMACY

If you dream that you keep trying to get intimate with your spouse but you are struggling, it could indicate your own spiritual struggle to get into an intimate relationship with the Lord. The Lord is trying to let you know that there are so many distractions in your life right now that you are struggling to come closer.

There are just too many voices and responsibilities that keep pulling you in so many directions, that your very relationship with the Lord is starting to suffer.

You need to learn to be honest and real with yourself. Dreams are there to give you direction and sure, when you are interpreting for others, now is not the time to expose all your shortcomings.

When you are ministering, it is the time to come across with confidence so that the person you are ministering to can have faith in you. However, when it comes to dealing with your own dreams and struggles, be honest with yourself and face your flesh, so that the Lord can give you what you need to overcome it.

6. DREAMING OF FLYING

When I looked at this symbol when I wrote the symbol dictionary, He gave me such a clear picture. King David shares in the Psalms saying that if only he could be a dove that he would fly to the wilderness. When I read that scripture, all my flying dreams suddenly made sense.

If you dream of flying or trying to fly, it means that you are trying to escape. You are trying to escape the problems and pressure that you are facing right now. You need to determine if this is positive or not.

FLYING WITH FREEDOM

Perhaps you are flying high above the mountains and valleys and you are soaring with the clouds. In the dream you feel free and full of joy. This is a wonderful picture of how it is in the realm of the spirit. The Word says that we are seated in heavenly places with the Lord.

The Lord is saying that you can fly high above your problems. This speaks of walking in freedom, high above your cares. You can see things from His perspective and you do not need to become bogged down with the cares of this life. After those dreams, you wake up fantastic.

The Lord is telling you to look at things from His perspective. You can escape the problems of life if you run into His arms. He is far above the problems you are having and with Him you can soar like an eagle.

CANNOT GET OFF GROUND

On the other hand, you have these dreams where you keep trying to fly, but you cannot seem to get off the ground. You are running and jumping and trying to fly, but you keep crashing down. This dream means that you are trying to escape the problems of life, but that they are overcoming you.

You need to discern if you are just trying to run away from your problems in life because you do not want to face it, or if the problems are actually overwhelming you. I am more inclined to believe the former interpretation.

PEOPLE CHASING YOU

If you keep trying to jump or run or fly away from people that you are chasing you, the best thing that you can do in your dream is to stop and face those people.

It could be that right now there are pressures in your life that are coming on you and that you are trying to escape them. You feel so stressed and overwhelmed with these cares and you just want to run away from them. However, the only way to overcome is to stop and turn around and to deal with the pressures head-on. Only then can you soar like an eagle once again.

If you keep dreaming of trying to escape, then perhaps the Lord is telling you that it is time that you face your problems. You keep trying to find an easy way out or a back door, but He is not going to give it to you. If you are ever going to overcome these pressures, it will mean facing them and walking right through them.

At the time that King David wrote about flying away, Absalom was chasing him and he had pressures all around him. Running away was not a solution. It was only when he stopped and faced his enemy that he overcame. David did not run away from Goliath, but he faced him.

Had David not faced and overcome all of the pressures that came on him as king he would not have been the greatest one that ever lived.

You are not alone if you feel like you want to run away from your problems. However, there are times you have to turn around to face those problems

QUESTIONS FOR REVIEW

1. If you have a good relationship with your mother, what could she represent in your dreams?

   _____

   _____

2. If you have a good relationship with your father, who is he likely to represent in your dreams?

   _____

   _____

3. If you have a good relationship with your spouse, whom would he/she represent in your dreams?

   _____

   _____

4. Can you think of a person that would represent the Holy Spirit in your dreams?

   _____

   _____

PRACTICAL PROJECT: BREAKING DOWN THE CHARACTERS

Apply this project to your own dreams. Take the characters of your own dream in the previous practical project and next to each character write:

1. Your relationship with that person. Whether positive or negative.
2. If you had to describe them using one or two words, what words would you use?
3. Is this a character you dream of often? (If yes, then they represent a part of yourself and your life).
4. Is this character an unidentified lady? (If yes, she could represent your feminine/creative/prophetic side).
5. Is this character an unidentified man? (He could represent your masculine/intellectual/teaching side).

As you identify each character, your dream will immediately begin to make sense. Above all else ask the Lord for wisdom and revelation to help you identify the characters in your dream. As you identify each one you will look back on past dreams and will notice how even back there the Lord was speaking to you of events that took place in your spiritual walk!

Character:	One/two word description:	
Relationship with character:		
Emotion: ○ Positive ○ Negative	**Gender:** ○ Male ○ Female	**You dream of person:** ○ Seldom ○ Frequently
What the character represents:		
Extra Notes:		

Character:	One/two word description:

Relationship with character:

Emotion:	Gender:	You dream of person:
o Positive o Negative	o Male o Female	o Seldom o Frequently

What the character represents:

Extra Notes:

Character:	One/two word description:

Relationship with character:

Emotion:	Gender:	You dream of person:
o Positive o Negative	o Male o Female	o Seldom o Frequently

What the character represents:

Extra Notes:

Character:	One/two word description:

Relationship with character:

Emotion:	Gender:	You dream of person:
○ Positive	○ Male	○ Seldom
○ Negative	○ Female	○ Frequently

What the character represents:

Extra Notes:

Character:	One/two word description:

Relationship with character:

Emotion:	Gender:	You dream of person:
○ Positive	○ Male	○ Seldom
○ Negative	○ Female	○ Frequently

What the character represents:

Extra Notes:

EXERCISE

Apply this exercise to those who bring their dreams to you for interpretation. In looking at the person's personal life, here are some suggestions for you to identify what the characters in their dreams speak of.

1. **What is the relationship with the character in real life?**

   _____

   _____

   _____

2. **When they bring this person to their mind, what is the first impression that they receive of this person?**

   _____

   _____

3. **Is this a character they dream about often? If so, then this character will always represent that same part of them.**

   _____

   _____

4. **If they had to give you a few words to describe this character in real life, what would be the words they would use? E.g. - dominating, loving, gentle, kind, good with money, selfish, bitter, worldly, intellectual, strong in faith, strong in hope, hard worker, deceiver, gossip, encourager… you get the idea!**

   _____

As you take the descriptions of the characters you will begin seeing a pattern. Take this application and apply it personally to this person's life. For example, if they are dreaming of a friend who is bitter, a deceiver, and a gossip, that friend could be a representation of their own sinful flesh.

If they dream of their father who is strong, kind, and a hard worker, he could represent the Lord in their own lives.

EXTRA NOTES

Lesson 13 - Gender and Race in Dreams and Visions

Based on: *The Way of Dreams and Visions*, Chapter 13

Looking at some more symbols as well as a good study on objects and landscapes, your interpretations are coming along nicely.

You might need to mark these pages with notes from your own experiences. The Lord will clarify what your symbols mean, but you need a starting point. These teachings give you just that!

They will tell you the direction you need to begin looking in, to get the full picture! So, here are a few more symbols for you to look at.

7. HAIR

Perhaps this is a woman thing. We are always stressing about our hair. Before I preach or need to do a lecture on camera, the thing that takes me the longest is always my hair!

Hair is a very part of a woman's image. This is not only relevant to our culture today, but it was always important since the time God created Eve. The Scripture speaks of how the woman is the glory of the man just as her hair is a glory to her.

It says that it is a shame for a woman to have a bald head, using that as an illustration for a woman without spiritual covering.

So when a woman dreams of her hair. The first thing it is speaking of is your image. When you change your hair, you change your whole appearance.

So when you dream of changes in your hair, the Lord is saying that He is taking you through a change of image.

He is saying that He is going to change who you are and change the way you view the world.

Most importantly though, hair is a picture of your covering. If you dreamed that your hair was being shaved, it would mean that you are not under the covering of your husband or your spiritual leader.

If you are married woman, my first interpretation would mean that you are not under the covering of your husband.

The interpretation is the same if you dream your hair is falling out or being cut off. There is something wrong with your covering! Either you are not under cover, or there is something wrong with the covering you are under.

MAN WITH LONG HAIR

For a man, their hair also speaks of their image. In fact, I know some men who are even more fussy about their hair than women are. So if you are a man and dream that you suddenly have long hair, this is not a good interpretation. In the New Testament a man was discouraged from having long hair.

It could be that the Lord is saying that your image is perhaps too feminine. You need to change your image.

GOING BALD (MEN)

On the other hand, that your hair is falling out, it means that you are not under covering. However, if you have a fear of going bald in the natural, then losing your hair is a reflection of your inner fears.

8. KEY

When I give someone the key to my front door, I am giving them license and access to anything in my house. We had a tradition in South Africa where on your 21st birthday you get a golden key. It is usually presented in a nice box and it is a symbolic picture.

It is the key to the house. In South Africa at 21, you are officially regarded as an adult, so when you receive this key, it is an announcement that you are of age and now have the key and license to the house.

Just as in our cultures a key speaks of authority, so does it in the Spirit as well. There is the prophetic key, but also other kinds of keys mentioned in scriptures.

When we see a brass key in the Spirit, it often speaks of a teaching ministry. I have seen the apostolic key as a jewel encrusted key.

LOSING YOUR KEY

Now what if you dream of losing your key or if someone steals your key. This is not good! It means that you are giving your license away. Now if satan has your key it is not good. It means that he has been given license in your life and you need to take it back.

You have given him access to your life and it is time to close that door and rise up in your authority again. So whenever you see keys in the Spirit or in your dreams, discern what kind of authority is being spoken about.

Across the board, it is speaking of authority and license. However, the kind of key it is or the context of the dream will tell you exactly what kind of authority you are talking about.

Now sometimes people have a dream of a key that looks like a fish. That sounds evangelistic to me. It speaks of an evangelistic authority. Use wisdom.

AT THE END OF THE DAY

I can tell you what the symbols mean and I can explain to you what I feel they are, but at the end of the day, it is for the Holy Spirit to give revelation and wisdom.

It is great to gather the knowledge in your head and you could study all of the symbols, but until you get wisdom and revelation to apply the interpretation, it means nothing.

So it is good that you are studying the principles, but once you have learned everything that you can and done everything that you can, it is time to put it all away.

Forget it all. Then flow out from your spirit and allow the Holy Spirit to direct you.

QUESTIONS FOR REVIEW

1. What are the two gender characters called that are common in our dreams?

_____

_____

2. How would your race or culture effect an internal dream interpretation?

_____

_____

_____

_____

_____

3. What is your doctrinal stand and can you identify common symbols related to your beliefs in your dreams?

_____

_____

_____

_____

4. Can you identify the female and male counterparts in your dreams?

_____

_____

_____

_____

PRACTICAL PROJECT

Now apply the principles to your own dream. Take the list of objects, landscapes and colors from your own dream in the previous lesson and write next to each one:

1. Is this object, landscape or color familiar to you?

Object/Color/Landscape:	Familiar/Unfamiliar:

2. **How did the object, landscape or color make you feel? Negative or positive?**

Object/Color/Landscape:	Negative/Positive:

3. **Is this object something you like, dislike, or are indifferent about?**

Object/Color/Landscape:	Like/Dislike/Indifferent:

4. **What are your first impressions when you think of this object, landscape, or color?**

Object/Color/Landscape:	First impression:

As you put these together you will very likely have a full interpretation of your dream. Do not be concerned if you find it more difficult to interpret your own dreams than the dreams of others. It is always God's order for us to use the gifts on behalf of others first. It would be a tremendous help for you to study this along with a friend so that you can share your dreams and revelations with one another.

EXERCISE

Before interpreting the symbols and circumstances surrounding the dreams of an individual it is important that you have a bit of background information on them. You will need to know:

1. **Their race and culture.** This is vital when they dream of characters familiar or unfamiliar to their social group. I had a dream to interpret where the person was dreaming negatively of black characters in her dream, yet she was black herself. If I had not known this, I would have given a totally incorrect interpretation. Knowing their culture will also explain the use of certain objects and symbols.

2. **What is the person's doctrinal stand?** For example, if they believe in Word of Faith, or in Catholicism they will dream of objects and symbols that line up with that doctrine.

EXTRA NOTES

LESSON 14 - EXAMPLES OF GENDER AND RACE

Based on: *The Way of Dreams and Visions,* Chapter 14

For the final lesson on this part, I want to include the symbols for Man and Woman from *The Dreams and Visions Symbol Dictionary,* to expand a little on the topic of "Gender" that I taught in *The Way of Dreams and Visions.*

MAN

As an unknown figure in your dream or vision a man typically represents your masculine (animus) or intellectual side. In ministry it speaks of a teaching orientation.

CHARACTER SPECIFIC SYMBOL

A man you know: It is important to identify what the character in the dream means to you. If this is a man you know well, what do you think he symbolizes in your life?

Spiritual father: If he is a spiritual father to you, then he could speak of the Lord in your dreams.

Friend: If he is a friend from the past, identify what characteristic stands out to you the most about this person.

If he is a close friend that you often rely on when you need help, he can be a picture of the Holy Spirit to you.

Famous: Furthermore, if you dream of an actor or public figure, consider what he stands for. (This also applies to a woman character). It is common to dream of a famous character such as the president, actor or a pastor. What does this actor represent to you? What is their most outstanding characteristic? (Please note that if you are always dreaming of actors and having "movie" dreams this is simply an indication that you are filling your mind too much with what is in the world. You need to do some cleansing and feed things into your spirit that edifies!)

President: Now when you have a dream of such a person, instead of applying the dream directly to them, consider what they would represent. A president could be a representation of the World System or Government System.

A pastor in your dream, depending on your relationship with that pastor, could represent the church system or even the Lord's work in your life.

An unknown man: A familiar but unknown male character in an internal dream often speaks of your masculine side - the animus. This side is left-brained, analytical, and logical.

Spiritually speaking, a man in your dreams often represents a teaching function. Perhaps you might dream that you are embracing this strange man. This would mean that the Lord desires you to embrace your teaching orientation.

Perhaps you dream that a man that you are familiar with in your dream, but do not know in real life dies. This would mean that your analytical nature is being brought to death.

If the Lord has been leading you into a teaching orientation in ministry, you might dream of meeting or marrying a man that you feel comfortable with, but do not know in real life.

This dream would confirm your direction in moving towards a teaching function.

Review the <u>Woman</u> symbol for an all-round look at the animus and anima.

UNIVERSAL SYMBOL

POSITIVE

If you see a man in vision, you will likely see someone you know, if they are a real person.

If you are in intercession, then you will likely see a person to direct your prayers towards. This person may actually look like you see in vision, or the vision you see may simply be a representation of what they stand for.

Take Paul's experience with the Macedonian that appeared to him in a dream telling him to come to them. Now the person he saw was not an actual person, but he represented the Macedonian people.

When I see demons or angels in the spirit, they are always masculine in gender. Depending on the level of demon, I will see various forms.

In the case of Paul, the Macedonian he saw was a positive vision. Consider what the man in your vision or external dream is wearing:

> *Acts 16:9 And a vision appeared to Paul in the night. A* **man** *of Macedonia stood and pleaded with him, saying, "Come over to Macedonia and help us.*

NEGATIVE

A vision of a negative man in Scripture would be Goliath. I have often seen a "spiritual Goliath" in vision.

Goliath represents the spirit of fear, and the Lord often leads me in intercession to break his stronghold over the lives of God's people.

Just take a look at what kind of influence Goliath had on God's people:

> *1 Samuel 17:24 And all the **men** of Israel, when they saw the **man**, fled from him and were dreadfully afraid.*

Goliath also represents your own fears that prevent you from rising up and moving forward.

WOMAN

Your more creative and prophetic side. Represents either your artistic nature or your prophetic call (if you should have one).

Positive:

- Your "right brained" functions
- Your ability to hear God's voice and flow in the spirit

Negative:

- To deliberately indulge in sin, knowing it is wrong

CHARACTER SPECIFIC SYMBOL

POSITIVE

You may at times dream of a woman that is familiar in your dreams, but in reality you do not know them.

As I teach in *The Way of Dreams and Visions*, a familiar feminine character in your dreams often represents your animas - your feminine side. This side is artistic, creative, prophetic and totally allegorical.

In a positive dream you might dream that you are embracing this lady. Some men who have shared such dreams with me felt guilty that they were embracing this woman in their dreams.

But the dream was actually positive, because it meant that the Lord was leading them into a more prophetic orientation or He was telling them that they need to tap into their creativity.

This also applies to women. As a woman you might dream that you are befriending this women character in your dream; perhaps even embracing her.

This DOES NOT mean that you have homosexual tendencies! It simply means that you are moving more towards a prophetic orientation.

NEGATIVE

Depending on how you respond to this feminine character in your dream it could mean different things.

If you are ignoring her, it could mean that you have been ignoring your prophetic side and the Lord wants you to get back to it.

Perhaps in your dream she is killed, which could mean that the Lord is bringing the prophetic in you to death, so that you can move on to the masculine, teaching orientation.

You must identify what you sensed in the dream and what witnesses in your spirit.

UNIVERSAL SYMBOL

POSITIVE

Depending on the context of your vision, seeing a woman will have a different meaning.

If it is a woman you know, then the vision relates to her. If it is a woman you do not know, then she could represent something.

A pregnant woman refers to something new that is about to be birthed. Depending on the direction of your prayer at the time, the birth could refer to the ministry, church or person you were praying for.

Of course seeing a bride speaks of the Bride of Christ. Depending on how you see her, will give you the full interpretation.

A bride standing in splendor would speak of the plan the Lord has for His church. A bride whose garments are tattered speaks of the church being in a state of disarray and needing mending.

NEGATIVE

A woman dressed in scarlet has a negative connotation according to this Scripture:

> Revelation 17:4 The **woman** was arrayed in purple and scarlet...
> 6 I saw the **woman**, drunk with the blood of the saints and with the blood of the martyrs of Jesus. And when I saw her, I marveled with great amazement.

This speaks of an adulteress and something that is seducing you to turn your back on the things of God. It means you are in adultery!

A woman that is a harlot or that you feel is very negative speaks of deliberately sinning and satisfying your flesh instead of walking in obedience.

> Proverbs 7:10 And there a **woman** met him, With the attire of a harlot, and a crafty heart.

Witch: If you see a woman that looks like a witch, it can have a variety of meanings. It can speak of witchcraft specifically, however in my experience, this is how I see the Jezebel spirit. It speaks of an aggressive nature that seeks to dominate and control through manipulation and guilt.

QUESTIONS FOR REVIEW

1. What is the standard for all prophetic revelation?

   _____

   _____

2. What 3 natural characteristics do not apply to prophetic revelation as they did to internal dream interpretation?

   _____

   _____

   _____

   _____

3. Who is the source of all wisdom?

   _____

   _____

4. What is your ultimate goal in conversing with the Lord?

   _____

   _____

   _____

5. Do you desire to speak with the Lord face to face? You can! Submit yourself to Him now and ask that His Spirit move over you and change your life!

PRACTICAL PROJECT

You will now put the interpretation together for your own dream. As before you will journal it. But before you even start, ask the Lord for His wisdom and understanding. Ask Him to minister to you through this interpretation. Do not see this as just "something of interest," but as a tool to receive direction, encouragement and counsel from the Lord.

1. Begin by asking the Lord for revelation. Opening your heart to Him.

2. Share any concerns that you have on your heart and clear your conscience before Him.

3. Ask the Lord to give you the interpretation for this dream and to give you wisdom.

4. Then begin by summarizing your dream in your own words. You may receive the interpretation through a prophecy, where the Lord is speaking to you directly, but if you feel you are not ready for this just yet, just begin by writing down the summary in your own words.

5. Let the words flow out of your spirit.

6. Ask the Lord questions as you think of them and then answer those questions with what you feel coming up from within. Do not be alarmed if the answers sound like you – they are meant to, because they are coming up out of your own spirit.

7. You will learn soon enough how to discern what is of the Lord and what is not with practice.

Spend additional time in the presence of the Lord and looking into the word for a complete answer. As you seek Him, He will not let you down but answer your very desire!

_____

_____

_____

_____

_____

_____

_____

_____

_____

_____

_____

EXERCISE: PUTTING IT TOGETHER

Now you must put all that you have received from those who submitted their dreams to you together. Earlier you were asked to journal and to learn how to flow from your spirit.

Now this is the part of the interpretation where you put your mind out of the picture and allow the Holy Spirit to help you.

It is not good enough to simply give an interpretation, you must also learn how to use the interpretation to minister and to give this person direction. So do not stop at the interpretation but take it now a step further!

1. Find a quiet place and put aside all the notes you have made of the person's dream.

2. Now going by memory alone, begin writing the interpretation out as if you were documenting your results.

3. As you do this it is very likely that you will see things that you missed before. Keep going! It means that the Holy Spirit is giving you revelation.

4. Now as you complete the interpretation you will have an idea of what the dream is saying.

5. Perhaps the dream indicates that this person is under spiritual attack. Or perhaps that they need to go in a certain direction. It might even be highlighting an area of their lives that needs dealing with.

6. Now you must turn this into a ministry opportunity! End by praying for this person. If they are under attack, come against the enemy. If they need encouragement speak blessing on them. If they need direction, speak wisdom.

7. Once again let the revelation flow from within, you will find yourself speaking out things that you did not plan on saying. This is the Lord, so keep pouring out until you 'run out of words' so to speak.

As you keep applying this you will begin seeing fruit in those you are ministering to. Your revelation will also increase as you look to the Lord and as others look to you for direction.

GROUP PROJECT

Allow time for everyone in the group to share characters and symbols in their dreams that they could not identify themselves. Ask them these simple questions:

   a. What is the first word that comes to your mind right now when you think about this person?
   b. What kind of relationship did you have with this person in the past?
   c. What kind of relationship do you have with this person now?
   d. Do you feel that they are a positive, negative or neutral picture to you?

If the symbol that the person cannot identify is a place or building, ask the following questions:

   a. Is this a building that you are familiar with (i.e. from your past)?
   b. In the dream, who does the building belong to?
   c. What emotions does this building bring up in you?
   d. Does this building remind you of anything in particular?

For external prophetic dreams, you will need to look into the Word for solutions. However, by getting the person to speak about and identify the characters and places, things will already begin to fall into place for them.

Copyright © Apostolic Movement International, LLC

EXTRA NOTES

PART 05

EXPERIENCING THE REALM OF THE SPIRIT

PART 05 - EXPERIENCING THE REALM OF THE SPIRIT

KEY PRINCIPLE

Do you want to bring change in your church? Start on your face before the Lord, asking for a revelation of the love of Jesus Christ!

LESSON 15 - EXPERIENCING THE REALM OF THE SPIRIT

Based on: *The Way of Dreams and Visions*, Chapter 15

MAPPING OUT PERSONAL MINISTRY

Switzerland is most famous for its chocolate and its watches. However, having been there a few times, I have come to see it as more famous for its road works and its detours. Never in your life have you ever seen anything like a detour in Switzerland.

I will give them this one grace - their detours are well laid out. There was one occasion when we had a conference and as it often happens, we were running late. So we had to rush to get there on time. The place we had to be was quite a distance away and so we were pushing the bounds of the speed limits.

However, what do you know one of those famous detours were being signaled right up ahead of us. Now if you have ever traveled a bit in Europe you will know what I am talking about, when I describe it as a network of narrow roads and a network of fields. This was an experience I would never forget.

We were led off the main road and turned into a side road of a side road. Then led further into another side road. That led onto a dirt road and onto another road that did not have a name until I was seeing parts of Switzerland I never knew existed.

Things got worse. We hung faithfully onto each sign we saw the end of each bumpy road. Following the arrows, we eventually landed up in the middle of a field where the corn was so high on either side of the car that you could not see out.

Going at a snail's pace by now, Craig and I looked at each other thinking, "Ok, is this even a road?" Just as we were losing hope, we looked up and saw something in the distance. Yep, it was another poor soul thinking the same thing we were.

So we plucked up our courage and kept going until we saw the next little sign. Eventually through the process of intercession and a heavenly miracle, we did find our way to our meeting.

The point is, had it not been for all the signs along the way, we would still be trying to find our way home. It would have been impossible to memorize a route like that.

Now experiencing the world of the spirit is a bit like that sometimes. When you come to prayer or personal ministry, you might have an idea in your mind of the direction you think that you need to go. However, as you start out, you get a detour and the Lord starts showing you things that you really did not expect.

LEARNING TO READ THE SIGNS

Well what are you going to do about it? The most important thing to do naturally, is to learn to read the signs.

When you are ministering and the Lord gives you a vision, the symbols in those visions are like road signs, leading you to the correct destination. They will tell you which way to go. Just like a detour leads you to one sign at a time, the Lord will do the same thing.

No detour gives you a fully laid out map of where you are headed. No, you just get an arrow here or there. It is the same with the Lord. As you stand to minister, He is not going to give you the full map before you head out. Instead He will give you a sign here and there and all that you need to do is follow those signs.

It is simple really, and takes so much pressure off the entire process. Before you minister, preach, counsel or even pray for healing, you really do not have to get the full picture of what God wants to do. Do you think Moses knew the full picture when God called him?

Paul had no idea of all the great things that He would do. Little did Solomon know that he would be doing a lot more than just building the temple. No, the Lord unfolded his plan like those detour signs.

Sometimes they lead in a way that you do not understand, but if you are faithful to follow that sign, another will follow. What you are about to learn in the next 4 lessons is how to identify and interpret these signs so that you can be confident that you did everything God wanted you to.

QUESTIONS FOR REVIEW

1. What was the most devastating thing that Adam and Eve lost when they were expelled from the Garden of Eden?

   _____

   _____

2. What made it possible for us to enter once again into direct communication with God?

   _____

   _____

3. What are the three categories of vision?

   _____

   _____

4. Why was it necessary for the Lord to use trance and open visions to get His message through to the Old Testament prophets?

   _____

   _____

   _____

PRACTICAL PROJECT: HEARING FROM GOD

The easiest way to hear from the Lord is through vision! You do not need to be an Old or New Testament prophet to see visions or hear from the Lord, all you need to do is desire it! So, your project this week is going to be to receive a vision from the Lord!

1. Find a quiet place where you will not be interrupted.

2. Spend some time in the Word reading through your favorite passage or praising the Lord with your favorite songs.

3. Make sure you have a pen and paper on hand.

4. Now as you worship the Lord, close your eyes and take note of any pictures that "flash" in your mind.

5. Do not try to interpret or discern these visions for now, just become aware of them. Yes, some of them will be your imagination, but some will be of the Lord.

6. Those pictures that come back repeatedly and gently are the ones you want to take note of!

7. You might get one picture or you might get a whole lot!

8. Write down each picture you see in your mind.

In the next project I will teach you how to sort the junk from the revelation so that you can begin discerning for yourself when the Lord is speaking to you!

PICTURES:
___
___
___
___
___

_____
_____
_____
_____
_____
_____
_____

EXERCISE: IDENTIFYING VISIONS

Below are three examples of visions. One is an impression on the mind, the other a trance and the other an open vision. Read through each one and apply the principles shared in this chapter by identifying each one. Then answer the questions after each one. Look at my answers at the back of the book afterwards and see if you were correct!

Each of these examples have been taken from the Word.

> ### VISION 1: "The Candlestick"
>
> Now the angel who talked with me came back and wakened me, as a man who is wakened out of his sleep. 2 And he said to me, "What do you see?" So I said, "I am looking, and there is a lampstand of solid gold with a bowl on top of it, and on the stand seven lamps with seven pipes to the seven lamps. 3 Two olive trees are by it, one at the right of the bowl and the other at its left."
>
> Zachariah 4:1-3
>
>

QUESTIONS:

1. **What type of vision is this?**

   - Impression on the mind
   - Trance vision
   - Open vision

2. **Why do you think it is this type of vision?**

   _____

   _____

   _____

> **VISION 2: "The Dove"**
>
> And John bore witness, saying, "I saw the Spirit descending from heaven like a dove, and He remained upon Him. 33 I did not know Him, but He who sent me to baptize with water said to me, 'Upon whom you see the Spirit descending, and remaining on Him, this is He who baptizes with the Holy Spirit.'"
>
> John 1: 32-33
>
>

QUESTIONS:

1. **What type of vision is this?**

   - Impression on the mind
   - Trance vision
   - Open vision

2. Why do you think it is this type of vision?

_____

_____

_____

> **VISION 3: "Glory of God"**
>
> But he (Steven), being full of the Holy Spirit, gazed into heaven and saw the glory of God, and Jesus standing at the right hand of God, 56 and said, "Look! I see the heavens opened and the Son of Man standing at the right hand of God!"
>
> Acts 7: 55-56

QUESTIONS:

1. What type of vision is this?

    o Impression on the mind
    o Trance vision
    o Open vision

2. Why do you think it is this type of vision?

_____

_____

_____

EXTRA NOTES

Lesson 16 - Visions and Warfare

Based on: *The Way of Dreams and Visions*, Chapter 16

You are headed for disappointment if you think that the one revelation you have is the complete picture. No, your revelation is just one stage of your journey. When you can come to terms with that, you will see that the Lord has more revelations for you and together they will piece the full message together as a puzzle.

Holding onto a single revelation would be like us driving into the middle of that corn field and saying, "Yep this must be it! It is where the sign sent us, so clearly we have arrived at the meeting place." Do not be daft… you are in the middle of nowhere. It is clear you have not arrived at your destination yet.

You have to keep going, and the great thing about the Holy Spirit is that he will give you confirmation of your direction. If you have ever given a prophetic word, then you know what I am talking about. The Lord will give you the first picture or sentence and will not give you the rest until you have shared that.

FOLLOWING THE SIGNS IN PERSONAL MINISTRY

You might not be ready for the full picture yet, so it is important that you follow the signs along the way. This is especially important in personal ministry. You can spend hours ministering to someone at times and only near the end do you get the full revelation of the root of their problem.

Sometimes I want to fight with the Lord about that. I want to say to the Lord, "Why didn't you give me this full revelation at the beginning? Why did you wait so long? Why did I have to go through the corn fields before reaching my destination?"

UNFOLDING THE REVELATION

I have come to realize that the person is not ready for the final revelation. He knows what is in their hearts and what it will take to prepare them to deal with what He is trying to expose. The Lord is gracious like that. He gives them time to rest and open their hearts. He gives them time to trust Him and trust you.

So when you first start ministering to someone, the Lord will start by giving simple revelations and then He will lead into revelations that zero in closer to the problem, when that person is ready to receive.

So if you have had that kind of experience, do not feel like you failed. The point is that the person was not ready and the Lord will unfold the full revelation one step at a time.

INTERPRETING SYMBOLS IN VISIONS

I will be basing this chapter on some of my own personal experience. Perhaps as I share here, the light bulb will go off for you as you remember similar experiences in the Spirit.

Sometimes the interpretation to a symbol is easier than you think, and all you need is a confirmation of what God is saying.

So let me take you by the hand and give you the meaning to some common symbols that Craig and I have experienced in our own ministry.

TWO QUICK POINTS

Do you remember when I shared how everything is symbolic in an internal dream? Visions are completely different to that. If you see a particular person in a vision, they are not symbolic. The Lord is telling you to either pray for them, or that they are related to the ministry you are doing at the time.

This is a big different between dreams and visions.

The second thing you need to keep in mind is that your symbols will have their interpretation in the Word. Now this is not a hard and fast rule, because as you come to minister, it is likely that you will see symbols that are common to that person and that they might only know.

The Lord will give you a picture that they can relate to, so do not be arrogant and think you have all the answers as to what a symbol means, especially when it comes to personal ministry.

You might not be able to find a chapter and verse for that symbol, but the Lord will use it to get his message across.

At the end of the day though, the Word is our foundation. Too many prophets go on their feelings or what they think instead of on the solid truth of the Word. This will help you from slipping into deception.

The key then is to flow in both! To flow in the gifts of revelation and also in the Word. Do not stand up and share a revelation that is just a list of scriptures. This is over swinging. On the other hand, do not stand up with a list of "how you feel" without having any scriptural foundation.

As you continue to work through these teachings, you will find your balance. So if you are not there yet, do not get under pressure, because you will arrive!

QUESTIONS FOR REVIEW

1. Why is it so vital to see where the enemy is coming from in the spiritual realm?

   _____
   _____
   _____

2. Have you ever come into confrontation with demons of darkness?

   _____
   _____
   _____
   _____

3. Why will the representations of what a demon looks like change from one person to the next?

   _____
   _____
   _____
   _____

4. Is the enemy allowed to attack us any time he pleases?

   _____
   _____

PRACTICAL PROJECT: IDENTIFYING REAL VISIONS

You should have a list now of the pictures you saw from your last practical project. Pull these out again and go through them as we take a look at what is a vision and what is just your own mind.

- A vision from the Lord can either be in full color or black at white.
- It can either be moving and you can follow it, or it may come as still life flashes.
- The picture came to you repeatedly.
- When you tried to even put the picture out of your mind, it came back gently.
- You felt something "good" about this picture. You seemed drawn to it.
- The symbols and objects in your vision can be found and paralleled with the Word.

Take those pictures that you saw that apply to those points and do the following:

1. Take each picture and look it up in the Word (A good concordance on CD ROM is priceless for this exercise).
2. As you discover what each object represents, put it together in a summary.
3. Now see if you can link the pictures you saw together.
4. Is there a common theme?
5. Is there a specific message that seems to be coming across to you?

Picture:

Picture:

Picture:

Picture:

Picture:

Picture:

Congratulations! You have begun to hear from the Lord for yourself! As you continue to use these principles, seeing visions and seeing into the spiritual realm will be second nature to you!

EXERCISE: IDENTIFYING DEMONIC ATTACK

The enemy cannot attack you any time he pleases – as we have already covered in our nightmare chapter. So if you are having nightmares and are being attacked spiritually, then how can you identify that open door to the enemy and close it? Here is a very quick checklist for you to test any nightmares and obvious attacks against.

The best teaching I can personally recommend that covers the subject of curses, demonic attack, and how to break free would be: *The Strategies of War*. There I discuss how to identify all the curses I mention here and how to overcome them. Then for a full teaching on how the enemy works and how to use it against him, I recommend *Prophetic Warrior* and *Prophetic Counter Insurgence* (Volumes 5 and 6 in The Prophetic Field Guide Series).

1. GENERATIONAL CURSE:

- This is easy to recognize if you just had to look at your family members! The deception or attack is not only common to you but also to other family members.

- You share the same "misfortunes" with other family members. Often dating back to your grandparents and beyond. (e.g. - certain diseases, "bad luck," clumsiness, etc.)
- Family members have been involved in the occult, false religion or heresy.

Closing the door: Closing this door to the enemy is very simple. James 4:7 - *"Therefore submit to God. Resist the devil and he will flee from you."*

- ✓ Submit yourself to the Lord and clear your heart before Him.
- ✓ Then break all spiritual ties with your generations. It can be a simple prayer something along the lines: "Father I break all spiritual links with my parents and grandparents up until the fourth generation. Satan, I close this door on you in the name of Jesus and you will not have any more license in my life through this!"

2. PERSONAL SIN:

- If you have had any involvement with the occult, false religion, or heresy in your past, this is an open door to the enemy.
- The greater sins though that keeps the door open are such sins as pride, bitterness and fear!
- Fear most importantly is a WIDE open door to the enemy. It is the complete opposite to the force of love and will cripple your spiritual life! If fear is rampant then you opened the door yourself to a curse and you must close it!

Closing the door: Once again, you submit yourself to the Lord, repent and then tell the enemy to get out!

3. SIN THROUGH OBJECTS:

- If you are being attacked specifically at night, then it is likely that you have brought an object into your room that is contaminated with a curse.
- The greatest source of curses is found in publications, writings, letters, books... anything like that. Why? Because our words contain our spirit! That is why the use of words is so powerful in prayer, but unfortunately also just as devastating when released with a curse.
- I suggest you do a full look through your room and see what you have brought into it since the attacks began. You might be surprised at what you will find!

Closing the door: Very simply, if is was a gift or something that can still be used, pray over the object. Dedicate it to the Lord Jesus and tell the enemy to go! If the object is designed specifically for demonic worship such as Buddha or African statues and that sort of thing, you will need to get rid of it. Such "religious" artifacts, rosary beads and the like should also be disposed of.

4. SIN BY ASSOCIATION:

Now this one is the most subtle, but actually the most common. When you share with someone, perhaps minister with them or even pray with them, you open your heart to them. The Scriptures say that we are not to let any man lay hands on us suddenly. Jesus also said, that He opened his heart to no man, because he knew what was in man. Why is that? The reason is when you make contact with another human, you join your spirit to theirs. You sense what they are sensing.

Now if that person is under a curse or has a demonic stronghold in their life, you partake of that curse! By linking your spirit with theirs, you partake of their curse! It is common knowledge that to get blessed and anointed, you hang around anointed servants of God and it rubs off on you. Well the same applies to curses!

I cannot stress enough how important it is to break spiritual links with everyone you minister with. Especially if you move into intercession! When you intercede for someone, you link your spirit with theirs. You feel what they are feeling and if they do not fully break free of the bondage they are under, you will find yourself experiencing a backlash and coming under their attack. Anyone who has spent some time in intercession will witness to this one!

- Look for curses that have suddenly "appeared" in your life.
- Suddenly things in your home start to break down.
- You suddenly become ill for no reason.
- You begin losing money through either direct theft or unexpected expenses.
- There is sudden strife in your home. Strife between you and your spouse and you and your kids.
- You are suddenly attacked by a spirit of fear that you cannot control.

Closing the door: Identify when exactly these things started happening and you will be able to link it to someone you either ministered to or met recently. To close the door is as simple as applying James 4:7 again. Submit yourself to the Lord and break spiritual links with the person who is under oppression. Just renounce any contact with that curse, and tell the enemy to get out of your home! Then in turn speak blessing on this person so that they can also break free!

Above all else look to the Lord for revelation! Allow Him to speak to you and help you identify where the enemy has license, and then close those doors! Fill your mind and heart with the Word of God, and overcome the enemy with the sword of the spirit. As a child of God you have the Holy Spirit living inside of you! So stand up and use your authority in Christ!

EXTRA NOTES

LESSON 17 - DEVELOPING YOUR RELATIONSHIP WITH GOD

Based on: *The Way of Dreams and Visions*, Chapter 17

You cannot touch the subject of dreams and visions without moving into the realm of the prophetic. So for this lesson, I am going to focus specifically on the role of the prophet in office when ministering in vision.

If you have been called to be a prophet, this is hardly the final word on the subject, but it will put some pieces into place for you. I suggest working your way through the *Prophetic Field Guide Series* for full training.

If you are not a prophet, the following teaching will help you understand the realm of the spirit a bit more and also what is going on, if you see a prophet speaking over the lives of others!

RELEASING THE FIVEFOLD MINISTRIES (SOMETHING FOR THE PROPHETS)

Because one of your primary functions as a prophet is to help God's people to find their place in the church, it is possible that you will see symbols in the Spirit that will indicate what this place is.

This is something that the Lord uses me in often, so I am going to share my experience with you here. There are many prophets going around and guessing where people belong, but so much more is needed. Not only does the Lord need us to get revelation, but also to release them into these offices.

How could David or Saul be anointed as king of Samuel did not take the time to anoint them? Aaron could never have taken his place either if Moses had not anointed him into the office he carried out.

In the same way, the Lord will call you to release His people. Now as a prophet the Lord will use you in many ways. He will give you revelation to identify body ministries and spiritual gifts.

I am doing this mainly because there is not a lot of teaching on the subject available and also because this is one area that the Lord uses me in very often.

So here they are, some of the main symbols that I see when praying for someone's calling and how I apply that revelation as the Lord gives it to me. I pray that it inspires you and imparts something fresh to you. So that you can stand up as Samuel as well and put God's people into place!

As you go through each of these symbols I encourage you to seek confirmation before you just release someone. Just because you see this symbol for them does not mean they are ready yet. There have been many times when I see a golden key in the Spirit, but do not feel led to release that person for another year!

1. THE GOLDEN KEY

This is a very clear picture that speaks of the authority of the prophet. When I see the prophetic key, I know that the Lord wants to release someone into prophetic training. (I give lots of detail on this in *The Way of Dreams and Visions Symbol Dictionary*)

When I see this key, it looks simple, gold, and big. It stands out when I am ministering. Now when you see that, it does not mean that the person you are ministering to is in prophetic office already.

WHAT TO DO WITH IT

It could be that the Lord is asking you to release that person into prophetic training. When I see the prophetic key then I know that the person in front of me is ready for prophetic training and I will lay hands on them and release them.

Usually when I do this I feel the anointing and another one of my team will get confirmation. I also often get a prophetic word of decree that will confirm what the Lord is showing me in the Spirit.

A key in Scripture speaks of authority in general, so you need to discern what kind of authority you are seeing. This is where confirmation and wisdom is needed. Not every key you see in the Spirit means you are to release someone into prophetic training! So be discerning here.

However, whatever the key is, the Lord is telling you, as a prophet, to release through decree some kind of authority over the person you are ministering with.

2. SHEPHERDS STAFF

This one is pretty obvious to most and speaks of the ministry of the pastor. When I see this as I pray for someone, I know that the Lord is telling them that He wants to make them into a pastor.

The shepherds staff is such a beautiful picture because it symbolizes the entire function of the pastoral ministry. Now I am not talking about the position of leadership here. I am not referring to the administrative function that the pastor also carries out.

I am speaking solely of the ministry function of the pastor. Many see the pastor as a titled position, but it is not true. When the Scripture speaks about the shepherds of the flock, it is speaking about more than just a leadership position.

It is also speaking about a function. A function to protect and love the sheep. A function to feed and nurture the sheep. We have a teaching in Mp3 format called *The Work of the Ministry - A Pastoral Foundation* that gives a full picture of the ministerial function of this fivefold ministry. Expect it to challenge everything you thought about this significant fivefold ministry.

So if you see something like that in the Spirit, it could be that the Lord is telling you to release that person into pastoral training.

3. GOLDEN SWORD

When I see this, I know that the person I am ministering to is being called to a teaching ministry. This is the same sword in Scripture, that divides the soul and the spirit and the intent of the heart. The Word of God is indeed a double-edged sword, and it is the teacher that will wield it the most.

Something to remember about this one, is that I have found that the teacher training is the longest out of all of the fivefold. The reason, is that this involves a lot more than just some character changing. It involves learning through both knowledge and experience, and this takes time.

Teacher training is more intense than just facing death to your flesh. It involves both learning the Word and then living the Word. It involves experiencing the principles you will teach others. This is something that you can share with anyone you might feel led to call to teacher training.

Just be the Lord's vessel. You do not need to get complicated. Simply release what God is showing you. If you are praying for someone and you see the teacher sword, you just need to release them into it.

4. TRUMPET OR SILVER SWORD

The trumpet in bible times heralded the king! This is a lovely picture of the evangelistic ministry. Another symbol that goes along with this one is a golden bell. The evangelist is the herald, making noise for the king!

It is a fantastic picture. In bible times, the herald would come and blow his trumpet and so read out the decree of the king. It is a wonderful picture because the evangelist is not only called to the unsaved, but to believers as well. To get that attention, he is often loud.

He might be the one upsetting people and getting noticed. He is the one saying things that are not so politically correct. He wakes people up and ignites the fire in them.

If you feel that the Lord is wanting someone to go through evangelistic training, you can rest assured that this person is about to go through the worst phase of death they have ever known. This training is one of the most stripping trainings you can face.

So do not just walk around releasing people into training unless you get confirmation. This is why it is so important to work in a team and not be a solo player. The authority that you are releasing is real and the pressures that will come on that person are real.

The Holy Spirit will come upon them and begin to shape them for that call.

5. CROWN, SCEPTER AND MANTLE

The apostle is the last of the fivefold ministries and when I see a crowning ceremony with these symbols then I know that the Lord is speaking of an apostolic ministry.

There are some other things that we see, and so you cannot make a hard and fast rule here. Like I said, I am sharing my own experience to help you along. I have also seen the staff of Moses, a jewel encrusted key (The Key of David) or a blueprint that all speak of the apostolic ministry.

I do not step out and release anyone into this kind of ministry until I have received a clear confirmation in my own spirit and from someone else.

Ok, as a young prophet though I was not so restrained. When I first started flowing in the gifts of the spirit, I was so excited that I was releasing stuff everywhere! I was releasing everyone, going wild!

Talk about pendulum swinging. Do not laugh out loud too confidently... because you have been there yourself!

So do not be afraid to wait a little on the Lord before releasing people. It is just one symbol, so wait for the confirmation and further revelations.

USING THE SYMBOLS WITH WISDOM

I get really nervous when I hear someone say, "I saw lots of golden keys so I released them all into prophetic training!" I want to cringe! I think, "Chill out a little! Maybe everyone is a prophet or maybe you just like seeing the golden key!"

Take it a step at a time and use some wisdom. Sense what is in your spirit. Just because I see one of these symbols when I am ministering, does not mean I jump up and just start releasing people. I hear the voice of the Lord quietly in my spirit first.

I receive a deep knowing in my heart. So when I release that person, as I start speaking, other symbols start to follow.

GOING ON A JOURNEY

As I minister to someone in the Spirit, it is like I start out on a journey. I start walking along this road and I watch out for the signposts along the way. One says, "Go right" and I follow. Another one says, "Go left" and I follow.

Ministering in the Spirit is as simple as that, especially when it comes to identify people's callings.

A PRACTICAL EXAMPLE

Say someone comes to you for ministry or for confirmation of their calling. You pray and the Lord shows you one of the symbols we have covered so far. You feel in your spirit that the Lord wants you to release something.

So step out and lay your hands on the person and start to pray. Give the person to the Lord and thank the Lord for what you see, as you do this, more symbols or revelations will follow.

If this happens, then your journey has begun! You are headed in the right direction. Continue to pray what you see and what you feel until you come to the end of that road. You will know that it is time to finish when things suddenly get quiet in the Spirit and the Lord stops talking.

However, if you step out to pray and you feel like you got stuck or like there is cotton wool in your mouth, then politely bring the prayer to the end. Do not force it, because it is not yet time.

Simply speak a blessing on the person and then say amen. Do not try to push through if there is no sign. You will only end up in a ravine stuck in the mud somewhere!

Unfortunately, another weakness of the prophet is knowing when to shut up! We like to run and run even when no more detour signs have been given!

QUESTIONS FOR REVIEW

1. Why is seeing into the spiritual realm so powerful in praise and worship?

2. What does seeing into the spiritual realm accomplish when you are struggling in the natural?

3. Do you desire to move into a personal relationship with Jesus?

PRACTICAL PROJECT: THE GIFT OF DISCERNING OF SPIRITS

I cannot begin to describe the value of this God given gift to you! How important it is as believers to sense what is of the Lord and what is not.

1. **How many times have you been deceived by false revelation?**

   _____

   _____

   _____

2. **Are you able to tell the difference between anointed praise and worship and unanointed praise and worship?**

   _____

   _____

   _____

3. **Have you ever seen angels in the Spirit?**

   _____

   _____

   _____

4. **Have you ever seen demons in the Spirit?**

   _____

   _____

   _____

5. Can you tell when a preacher is speaking under the anointing?

_____

_____

_____

_____

6. Can you tell when someone is praying under the anointing?

_____

_____

_____

_____

If you can identify these experiences in your spiritual walk, then you have already begun to flow in this gift! If you would like a deeper experience of this gift or would like to receive it for the first time, I encourage you to reach out to the Lord right now and ask Him for it.

The Word says that if you ask for bread, he will not give a stone and if you ask him for a fish, He will not give you a scorpion. If you ask the Lord for a gift – He will NOT give you deception. So put your trust in Him now and reach out your hand in the Spirit.

See yourself before the Lord reaching out your hand. Now ask him in your own words for this gift. Tell Him of your desire and as I pray, you see the Lord Jesus giving it to you!

Lord I speak a spirit of revelation and wisdom on your servant. I ask that even now the gift of discerning of spirits would be imparted and released into them. In the name of Jesus, I call the gifts within to be released! May you see into the spiritual realm as never before! May you sense what is of the Lord and what is not!

May you know when God is moving and when He is not! May you feel the breath of the Holy Spirit on you and know when He is present. May you sense His wonderful spirit on praise and worship, the Word and all things that He has put His seal upon. Reach out now and know child of God, that He has answered your request and that a seed has been planted in your spirit even now! Expect to experience and move into this gift and know that the Lord will be faithful to meet you at His word and at your desire! Amen!

EXTRA NOTES

LESSON 18 - EDIFICATION OF THE BODY

Based on: *The Way of Dreams and Visions*, Chapter 18

This lesson is for everyone with a desire to help God's people. As you flow more in dreams and visions, the Lord will begin opening doors for you to minister. Did you know that all of the fivefold ministry (and many of the body ministries as well) flow in visions?

If the Lord has been leading you to counsel or motivate, then this lesson is just for you! As you step out and are used of the Lord in personal ministry, these principles will help you take what God is showing you and to minister to others.

SYMBOLS IN PERSONAL MINISTRY

There are certain symbols that you will see when in personal ministry that are pretty universal. If I had to say to you right now, "I see a vision of you in a prison."

I think that is pretty self-explanatory. Bondage is a universal concept that was understood 2000 years ago and is still well understood today.

So when I am praying for someone and I see them in a prison, I know exactly what that means. It means that they are bound by something. When I looked at this particular subject in the Word, I was amazed to see how often it is referred to.

1. A PRISON

A prison speaks of bondage no matter where you come from. It is also a very negative picture unless it is the enemy bound up in there. So if you are praying for someone and see them in a prison, you know that they are in bondage.

All you have now is the first picture though. You have your first sign along the journey. You do not know what the bondage is in their life or why they ended up in this spiritual condition.

You continue to pray for the person and now you see them in a cave, being chained to a wall. Again what is this saying? It is confirming that they are in bondage in some way. The chain is telling you that they are bound by the enemy.

The Lord does not bind us. Satan is the accuser and oppresses the saints. Now as you pray, you might also see that person at a specific age.

MINISTERING INNER HEALING

When I am ministering to someone and the Lord is leading us towards inner healing, these are the kinds of symbols that I see. I will see them restricted or bound in some way.

I can see that person is restricted, now I ask the Lord why they are restricted. Then as we pray about it or as I share their revelation I will see that person at a certain age. From there the Lord might expand the vision further.

I might see that person angry or crying. I might see them running into the cave hiding from everyone. Slowly a picture is unfolding that is bringing both you and the person you are ministering to an understanding of the root of their problem.

You realize that the reason that person is bound, is because they ran into that cave to escape the pressures or the rejection. They could not handle the hurt or whatever circumstance they were in at that age, and so they reacted by shutting themselves off to everyone.

Now that changes the revelation entirely. However, if you have just stuck with your first vision of the prison, you would never have received a full revelation.

At the beginning you realize that the enemy is binding them, but the reason that he is doing it is because they are the ones that ran away and shut off their hearts . They have given the enemy that license. Now they cannot break free.

You have a very clear first step to take. You cannot just go around dealing with demons. You are dealing with people and their hurts and problems are real.

As you identify the main source of their hurt, you can let them see that they have made some wrong choices in life. As you come to pray with this person, you might see something like a bleeding heart, and you can see that they are still hurting inside.

The Lord is letting you know that the conflict that they are experiencing right now relates to an era from the past. The Lord is not just showing you the problem, but the root of it, so that you can help this person be set free.

This person needs healing in their past to make them strong now. This is a powerful ministry, but all you need to do is follow the road signs.

Whether you are bringing a prophetic word or ministering, just follow the signs. When the revelation and visions stop, then you stop.

2. ROADS

Another symbol that I see often when someone comes to me for ministry, particularly for direction, is different kinds of roads. Perhaps this is something you can relate to. When we get together to pray for the ministry, we would always see the things that God has planned for us as a road.

Sometimes we would come to pray and we would see a mountain in our path. Not good. Then we know that we have to stand on the Word and tell that mountain to be removed.

There are other times, you come to pray and the road is broad and open. This is wonderful! The Lord is saying, "I have made your path broad."

You might see a road that has thorns or stones along the way. What do you think that means? Clearly the enemy is trying to lay a snare for you. He is the one to sow the tares in the field. This vision means that the enemy is up to his tricks.

If we see a wall built across our road, we know that the enemy is trying to block us.

I have even at times seen hurdles set up along the road, and then I know that there are a set of phases I need to go through.

The best thing that you can do when you get a vision like that when in personal ministry is just to share what you see. Pictures like this are pretty self-explanatory, so you do not need to get too deep.

When you are in the Spirit and you allow the Holy Spirit to take charge, you will not only get visions, but you will also receive the understanding.

Perhaps as I have shared, some of the visions you have received in the past have suddenly fallen into place.

When you have the mind of the spirit, it all makes sense.

3. MOUNTAINS

Mountains are not always negative if you see them in the Spirit. Sure, if I see a mountain in my road, blocking me, this is not something wonderful. It speaks of a blockage in my life.

However, there have been times when the Lord has taken me to a mountain and much like Moses was called, the Lord will say to me, "It is time to climb the mountain."

I share a lot on this in the *Moses Mandate*. It is a time of being separated from everyone, and going into the presence of the Lord. It is a time of letting things go so that the Lord can do something new in your life.

So if you are praying for someone and you see a mountain in the Spirit, then you need to sense if this is a good thing that God has put here or if something that the enemy has put there.

If it is of the Lord, then this speaks of a call to separate yourself into the Lord's presence. To go as Moses into the presence of the Lord.

Now this can be a very encouraging word to receive. You can let them know that if everything around them has suddenly died, that they do not need to panic! The Lord has just called them to the mountain.

4. RIVERS

Rivers are mentioned so much in the Word. Do yourself a favor and grab a concordance or an online bible and do a search on water and rivers. You will see that very often it speaks of the anointing or the spirit of the Lord.

I have often had it that someone will come to me saying that they feel blocked spiritually. As I pray, I will see a river that is all muddy. When I see this I know that there is a contamination in their spirit. The Word says that rivers of living water flow out of us.

So if that river is muddy, then there is something in it that is not of the Lord! It means that they have been feeding on something that has come into conflict with the spirit of the Lord inside of them.

The best thing to do would be to get into the Word, switch off the TV and to clean your spirit up! Suddenly that river will clear up and they will be able to get into His presence once again.

5. WALLS

I see walls a lot and often it speaks of a blockage. A wall in your road means that the enemy is blocking your way. A wall between a couple speaks of division and disunity.

When you see something like this, it is not good enough to just pray against it. This is going to need some real ministry and you will need to counsel that couple and help them overcome their conflicts.

QUESTIONS FOR REVIEW

1. How are visions used in Intercession?

2. Why is it that you find it easier to interpret for others instead of yourself?

3. How are visions used in counseling?

4. What is so powerful about using visions in physical healing?

___

5. What is the main reason for entering the realm of the spirit?

___

PRACTICAL PROJECT: LOOKING AT YOUR OWN LIFE

As the Lord has used you to minister to others, there needs to come a time when you allow Him to minister to you in this way also. Perhaps the Lord has been trying to get your attention concerning something. Perhaps there have been issues coming up from your past that need to be addressed and put to sleep. Now is the time to openly reveal these things and to give them over to the Lord.

1. Have there been past experiences, perhaps painful times, that have been coming to your mind recently?

___

2. When you sit down now to write, what past experiences immediately come to you?

_____

_____

_____

_____

_____

_____

_____

_____

3. What situations from this last week are coming to you?

_____

_____

_____

_____

_____

_____

_____

4. **Write each of these down as they come to your mind, and then do the following:**

- Give each hurtful or sinful memory to the Lord right now. See yourself handing that time over to Him.

- Ask the Lord to come and bring healing to your heart where it has been wounded. Allow Him to cover you now and touch you.

- Ask Him to forgive you of any sin you committed. Give Him your guilt and your fears.

- Then you tell the enemy that he has no right to accuse you any longer. That your sin is under the blood of Christ!

- If the memories that come to you are recent sins, simply repent and ask the Lord to cleanse you.

Now take this whole list of memories and go through each one in this manner. Then as you go through each one, you TEAR IT UP! This is the last time you will need to face that pain, the last time you will need to ask for forgiveness. That time of your life is over, history, under the blood! Praise the Lord for His wonderful grace and thank Him for His love. Now rest in that love and know that you are special to Him. Know that even now He is holding you gently in His arms and will never let you go!

EXERCISE: MOVING IN THE GIFTS

It is very likely that if you have been given the opportunity to minister for the Lord, that you have experienced some of the examples I shared in this book. Take a look now and identify how the Lord has used you by giving you revelation through visions and how you would further like to be used.

1. **Have you ever seen a spirit of infirmity when praying for someone?**

_____

_____

_____

2. Have you ever seen the organ or body part that is ill when praying for a person? Perhaps you thought it was your imagination!

3. When you got down to pray for someone that was on your heart, did you see them in vision in a specific situation that you knew you had to pray them out of?

4. When you were in church worshiping the Lord, have you ever seen angels of some kind of activity in the spiritual realm that indicated that the Holy Spirit was moving?

5. When ministering have you ever seen the person in question in a certain situation. Perhaps you saw an image of them when they were younger?

These are just a few examples of how the Lord can reveal through visions for the purpose of ministry. If you have been experiencing these already, then be encouraged and allow the Lord to mature this gift in you. If you have not operated in this way before then remain open to the leading of the Holy Spirit as He shows you new and wonderful things on behalf of others!

GROUP PROJECT

You have studied many symbols through this workshop so far, but now I am going to teach you the secret to finding the interpretations for yourself!

For this lesson, you need to have access to a good bible dictionary or, preferably a device with bible software on it that is searchable.

Everyone has their own preference, but it is beneficial to have a couple of bible versions for this project to be especially effective.

Once your group is together, do the following:

1. **Have each student mention at least one symbol that they have seen in a dream or vision that has not been covered in this workshop so far.**

   (It should be a symbol that cannot be found in *The Way of Dreams and Visions Symbol Dictionary* either – no cheating!)

2. **Make a list of the symbols and get ready to dig into the Word!**
   a. **Find the scriptural equivalent for your symbol.**

   For example, someone might have seen a light bulb in their vision. A scriptural equivalent would be a candle or a lamp.

   By finding the scriptural equivalent, you will have something to begin your search with! Get everyone to participate to find the correct symbol to research in the word.

   b. **Search that word in the Scripture**

   You will come across different scriptures, but as you work through each of them, a common theme will begin to come out.

   c. **Come to an agreement on what this symbol means and write the meaning down.**

d. **Work through each of the symbols together until you have a nice list together**
e. **You just started your own symbol dictionary!**

By digging into the Word yourself, you are reaching everyone to find their answers in the Word. Not only that, but you are truly studying the Word, without realizing it! You are painting pictures and making your spiritual foundation solid!

EXTRA NOTES

PART 06

INTERPRETING FOR OTHERS

Part 06 - Interpreting for Others

> *KEY PRINCIPLE*
>
> The most outstanding aspect of an internal dream is that you are the "star of the show."

Lesson 19 - Interpreting for Others

Based on: *The Way of Dreams and Visions*, Chapter 18 and 19

When I first got married, I not only got a crash course on how to cook, but also a crash course on how to fix cars. My husband had a little red Ford Escort. We called it the little red fire engine and although it was faithful, that faithfulness could only take us so far. Eventually a time came when things started falling and rusting off.

And so began our journey of learning our way around how a car works. I was amazed to find out how pistons were fired and how spark plugs sparked. I had a really good teacher in Craig!

Because Craig could not always fix it by himself, I was usually roped in as well.

Of course this was not always a positive experience. At one time Craig needed to take the entire engine out of the car. So he got a block and tackle, and he needed someone to operate it to lift the engine up out of the chassis.

So as he was getting the engine positioned, all I had to do was work that block and tackle. It was a strategic job, because we had to lower it in place correctly. So there I was, pulling away and lowering the engine. In the middle of my efforts, Craig says firmly, "Go!" I started going faster, but obviously not fast enough because he just kept on yelling at me saying, "Go! Go! Go!"

I was going as fast as my hands could move. All of a sudden he pulled away from the engine and was more than a little annoyed as he shouted, "What are you doing?! Are you trying to kill me?"

"What does it look like? I was going faster! You keep telling me to Go! Go! Go!"

"No I was NOT!" he answered out of breath. "I was saying WHOA! WHOA! WHOA!"

We were in mutual agreement after that day. My place was certainly not in his garage.

Now one of the first things my husband invested in was a good car manual for that model.

I was fascinated with this manual. If something went wrong, we could figure the problem out by picking up the manual and by following the instructions step by step. I thought to myself, "If only we had a manual like this for life."

Now as I am taking you through these teachings, that is exactly what I have tried to do. I have tried to give you the principles one step at a time and hopefully by now you are getting the hang of it.

Now as you come to ministering to people, there really is a simple course of action to follow. You never need to feel as if ministering is a hit and miss event. You do not need to fear that sometimes the Lord will talk to you and other times He will not.

You do not need to wander in the dark. You can hear from the Lord and apply what He gives you. If there are times when He does not talk, you can also know why and know what to do next.

Everything I share here, you can use in any kind of ministry. What I am doing in this teaching is giving you a manual to use and apply to your ministry.

Now the revelation and anointing are different. That comes directly from the Lord through your spirit. So what I am giving you here is a good structure to follow. I am giving you an understanding of how to approach someone in ministry and this allows the anointing that is already inside of you to flow out effectively.

So if I seem a little more logical than spiritual at times, I want you to know that it is intentional! Once I have grounded you in the nitty-gritty of ministry, you will receive the anointing along with it as well.

QUESTIONS FOR REVIEW

1. What are the 6 points to remember when ministering?

_____

_____

_____

2. Why is it so important to live each lesson you preach?

3. Why can't you interpret using your intellect?

4. What is the root for all ministry?

5. **Do you have what it takes to take on the responsibility of ministry in representing Jesus?**

_____

_____

_____

_____

PRACTICAL PROJECT: SEEING AS JESUS SEES

This is easy if you are used to walking in an intimate relationship with the Lord. People can be difficult to get along with and seeing them as Jesus sees them, is quite a task! So for your project this week, your aim is to see as Jesus sees!

1. Make a list of 10 people you know - beginning with those you DO NOT get along well with. (Hey, I am not going to make it too easy for you!)
2. Then daily, for a week, pray for each person on that list.
3. Speak the love of the Lord on them and speak blessing on them. Ask the Lord to open His doors of blessing on them.
4. Ask the Lord to show you each person as He sees them. Ask for wisdom and revelation.
5. See each person change from the way you see them now to the way the Lord sees them.

As you apply these simple yet powerful principles to your personal life, you will see people in a way you never thought possible. You will truly come to know the heart of the Lord Jesus and will then be in a position to show that heart to others in true love and transparency.

Name:

Revelation/Visions:

Results:

Name:

Revelation/Visions:

Results:

Name:

Revelation/Visions:

Results:

Name:

Revelation/Visions:

Results:

Name:
Revelation/Visions:
Results:
Name:
Revelation/Visions:
Results:

EXERCISE: MINISTERING IN LOVE

As people come to you for interpretations of their dreams and visions, or even for ministry, you will be reaching out to them as the Lord Jesus would. It is vital that they receive from the Lord when they come to you. It is a common mistake to think we already have the answers and know what is going through this person's mind – but no one knows that except the Lord Jesus Himself! Below is a list of points I want you to memorize and then apply to those who come to you for ministry:

1. **How does Jesus see this person?**

    Ask the Lord to show you this person through His eyes, so that you might know what is truly in their heart.

2. **How can I show this person Jesus?**

    Once you have been able to see them through the Lord's eyes you will see this person's need and desire. How would the Lord respond to this need?

3. **Put away all pre-conceived ideas.**

    This is especially important if you know this person personally. Put out of your mind everything you have known about them up until now. Treat them like they have come to you for ministry for the first time.

4. **Realize that you minister by FAITH and not need.**

    Unless the person coming to you is coming with a heart to receive you cannot minister. They must come with an open heart and the Lord will move on their behalf and give you what you need to minister.

5. **Always respond in love.**

    No matter what the Lord gives you or what you sense in the Spirit, always minister in love and understanding. Even if the person is out of order, respond out of concern. Even if a correction is given, if your heart is one of love – it is that very love that will win them over!

6. **Get Revelation!**

   Very importantly ask the Lord for revelation with regards to this person's needs. If you see a vision or hear any words, then share it with the person. Do not try to impose any revelation, but rather share it as you received it and give them the opportunity to see if it applies to them.

7. **Apply it!**

   Once the Lord has spoken, do not allow the person to leave without applying the revelation. If they are under attack, pray and release them. If they are bound in guilt, speak forgiveness. If they need encouragement, then encourage. If they need a word of direction or release, allow the Lord to speak it through you. Without applying the revelation is it like a seed that remains dead in the ground, bearing no fruit.

EXTRA NOTES

Lesson 20 - Interpreting Internal Dreams

Based on: *The Way of Dreams and Visions*, Chapter 19 and 20

Unlike our little miscommunication in the garage, as I shared in the previous lesson, you can get things right first time! There are just a few steps you can take, to make sure that you get the interpretation correct from the beginning.

There is nothing more embarrassing than running into an interpretation without listening to the full story! That is pretty much the story of my life! Someone will begin giving me instruction and I will run off in a hundred directions without hearing the final steps. Then I wonder why I end up flat on my face!

So take a page from my book of hard knocks. Follow these simple instructions when interpreting for others and you will find that you hit the mark every time!

HOW TO INTERPRET FOR OTHERS

1. LISTEN

Listen to what the person shares. Now that might not sound very profound. It might sound as obvious as opening that car manual and reading, "To start, open hood of car."

As simplistic as it might sound, you do not realize how necessary it is. The problem is that because you know so many principles, you do not even listen to what the person is really saying. You do not get the details, but jump straight into the conclusion.

Even if the person seems long winded, if you do not take the time to listen, you will not get all of the facts before acting on what you say.

2. CATEGORIZE IT

This will set the stage for your interpretation. That already gives you a direction to start going in. If it is internal, you are looking for symbols that represent a part of themselves. If it is a garbage dream you will not even waste your time interpreting it.

3. GATHER PERSONAL INFORMATION

This is especially important for internal dreams. Take the time to gather the information that you need to interpret correctly.

Are they familiar with the characters in their dream? Are the characters positive or negative to them? You cannot just guess these sorts of things.

If someone dreamed about their husband or wife, you cannot just guess what they mean to them. Take time to gather some personal information. Ask them a few questions.

1. How do you feel about this person?

2. Do you have a good relationship with them?

3. What is the first thought that comes to your mind when you think of this person?

4. IDENTIFY THE SYMBOLS

We have *The Way of Dreams and Visions Symbol Dictionary* to help you out there. Pick out their symbols and identify what they mean in the Word. By this point, you have your interpretation. It is laid out so perfectly for you.

5. BRING IT TOGETHER

It is great to know what the individual symbols mean, but it will only make sense when you bring it all together. You don't just give an interpretation and then leave it hanging. Ministry is meant to minister! So apply your interpretation and give the person hope to go on.

Sometimes we can get so hung up on what the symbols mean that we forget to minister. Do not give the person a long list of what their symbols mean. Move past that quickly and minister to the need and main point of their dream.

You do not make the person analyze their dream to the point that they analyze the Lord right out of it! These points are more for you to keep in your mind so that you have a track to run on.

Once you have all the information together, then you can bring it together and say what you feel God is saying. Then just before you end, you want give them something to do about it.

When Joseph interpreted the dreams for Pharaoh, he followed up the dream with some advice. He suggested that the grain was stored up. You must do the same thing when it comes to interpretation.

Do not say something like, "There is clearly an open door in your life and the enemy is attacking you." Great! How does that help? No, if the dream indicates that the person is under attack, follow that up by telling them how they can be set free.

Just because their dream shows that there is an open door, does not mean they are stuck. No, the Lord gave this revelation so that they can rise up and overcome.

If you apply each of these steps, you cannot go wrong. It is simple!

HOW TO START OUT

I find the best way to get started is by working with written dreams and visions. By doing this, you have the time to work through the dream and apply each of these steps correctly. It is not always so easy to do that when you have the person sitting expectantly in front of you!

When you have not had a lot of experience it is good to get people to write or email their dreams to you. In the beginning, you might find that you take longer than you would like, to put an interpretation together.

You might also find that you tend to get overly analytical, and think yourself into a corner. Do not get too stressed about that for now. Once you gain a bit of confidence, you will start to flow more out of your spirit than out of your head.

QUESTIONS FOR REVIEW

1. **What are the 3 points you will need to question a person on when interpreting their internal dream?**

   _____

   _____

   _____

2. **Why is it so important that you know the relationship the person having the dream has with the characters in their dream?**

   _____

   _____

   _____

3. If the objects in the dream are not familiar to the person, then what category of dream does it likely fall into?

_____

_____

_____

4. Why is it important to "sort out" the common from the uncommon objects and symbols in an internal prophetic dream?

_____

_____

_____

_____

EXERCISE: PRACTICAL EXAMPLE

By now you should have an idea how to identify a dream category, as well as the characters and objects in the dream. Next is an example for you to practice on. Identify the specifics, then write your interpretation of the dream. Complete your own interpretation before going on to read my interpretation.

> **THE KEY AND THE NEW DOOR**
>
> This dream was so real, that I could not sleep after I had it:
>
> I heard a voice say: "Stretch out your hands." So I did… and as I did, someone handed me a large, gold key that had rubies and diamonds encrusted on the handle area. Then the voice said: "Place the key in the lock of the door before you."

> I looked and there was now a door in front of me. So I put the key into the lock hole, and slowly turned the key, till I heard a loud "click."
>
> The door then opened. I looked inside and saw a place with no horizon! There was no ground below. But The voice said: "Step forward, in faith, and you will enter into the next level."
>
> Seeing that there was no ground to place my feet, I hesitated at first to step forward. But then I said: "I know you will be that bridge below my feet, Lord, so I may walk forward and not be afraid of falling."
>
> With that, I stepped forward. And as I did, even though I could not feel anything tangible under my feet, I did not fall! Then, as I continued to step forward, I began to see a sign that was way off in the distance. As I got closer, I could see that the sign said: "Welcome!" Then the voice said: "I have been waiting for you. Enter into this place of blessings."
>
>

Background information: This person is called to the apostolic ministry and often has prophetic dreams. Previous interpretations indicated a need to take action in the calling.

a) **Dream category:**

___

___

___

b) **Negative or positive:**

___

___

c) **Characters in the dream:**

_____

_____

_____

_____

d) **Objects in the dream:**

_____

_____

_____

_____

_____

_____

e) **Interpretation:**

_____

_____

_____

GROUP PROJECT

If you are able to have a time of praise and worship where you hold your meetings, then I suggest you begin this project by doing so. Continue until you feel the presence of the Lord.

1. When you feel the anointing, give your time to the Lord and invite Him to speak to you as a group.
2. Simply be open for anything that the Lord might say or do.
3. Encourage everyone to share any pictures that come to their mind, just as I teach in *The Way of Dreams and Visions* book.
4. As each student shares, encourage them further but concentrate on the pictures that are clearly from the Lord and apply them.

It is also a good idea to have a direction to pray for or perhaps something you can all bring to the Lord together. The Lord will only give revelation according to what you are asking Him for. It is a good idea to just bring the group to the Lord, and to ask if He has any direction or message for you as a group.

The object of this project is to teach the group to hear the voice of God. They should not be forced and if someone does not get anything, do not apply pressure. They might sense something or a scripture might come to mind.

The other objective is to get everyone comfortable and sharing what God gives them in a safe environment. For now, be patient and do not address any false revelation unless they completely disrupt the meeting.

EXTRA NOTES

PART 07

Spiritual Revelation and Discernment

Part 07 - Spiritual Revelation and Discernment

> **KEY PRINCIPLE**
>
> The Lord will always speak through His Word and His revelation will always back up His Word, and His Word will always back up His revelation. The two go hand in hand.

Lesson 21 - Revelation and Discernment

Based on: *The Way of Dreams and Visions*, Chapter 21

So, you ready for the final stretch? I suggest highlighting the steps in the previous lesson and taking time to memorize them for future use. Do the same for this lesson as we look at how to interpret visions for others.

Interpreting your own visions is a lot easier, because it often accompanies a word of knowledge. You will usually get some sort of impression as to what it means. When interpreting for others, you need to take a moment to listen to them share and then to sense in your own spirit what the Holy Spirit is saying.

Take note of these points and you will have a solid foundation to begin building on!

INTERPRETING VISIONS

1. LISTEN TO THE VISION

When you listen, try to separate the person's pre-conceived ideas from what God is really saying. What I often find when people have gone from place to place reading every teaching that they can get their hands on, is they end up with a strange mix of preconceived ideas.

Their vision tends to get colored because of this. There is a germ thought and a true revelation that God has given, but because they have fed so much other garbage into their minds, it becomes tainted. So when you are listening, you are trying to listen for the main concept of the vision.

The main meaning of the vision should be short, having a single message.

So try and sift through the junk. Sometimes I listen to someone's vision and think to myself, "Man! What have you been reading? A mixture of Harry Potter, the news, and the latest prophetic teaching that is circulating the Church?"

They need to get their heads out of the books and in the Word to bring about some balance. Now I am not saying that they are not getting revelation. The Lord really is talking to them. Unfortunately, though they are just piling on a lot of junk that was not really of the Lord.

This is where you will need to discern what is of the Lord and what isn't. You will find that some people will start out sharing a vision that is clearly of the Lord, and then it feels like something else kicks in and they go off on a tangent that is not of the Lord at all.

You will learn to hear when something has the right flow. You know the Lord Jesus and what His voice sounds like by now. So listen for that voice.

Another point to remember when you are listening to someone's vision is to hold off giving your own impression of their vision until they have shared theirs first. Do not jump in too eagerly to share what you think.

When someone receives a vision, they should have an idea of what it means. If they do not know what it means, they should have some kind of impression. It came out of their spirit after all! So give them their take on an interpretation before you give yours.

2. GATHER INFORMATION

You want to know what the person was praying for or doing at the time of receiving this vision. This is a vital step that you should not overlook. Visions do not fall out of the sky as you are walking along. They will come according to the flow you were in at the time.

If you had the vision while praying for your marriage, then the vision relates to that. Knowing this alone will make the interpretation come to light.

It will also make a lot more sense to you. So before you share your view, be sure to find out the context of their vision.

3. IDENTIFY THE SYMBOLS

In visions, all of the symbols will be based on the Word. By the time you have gathered the information and identified the symbols, the vision will fall nicely into place.

Keep in mind that visions are usually clear with a single message. You should not have a lot of symbols to interpret. Even if their vision seemed to have a lot of pictures, there should be one or two symbols that stand out the most in it.

These will give you the main emphasis of the message that the Lord is trying to convey.

QUESTIONS FOR REVIEW

1. What are the two kinds of visions can you receive?

   _____

   _____

2. What do you need to ask someone who has brought you their vision to interpret?

   _____

   _____

   _____

3. What is the difference between the internal and the external vision?

   _____

   _____

   _____

4. When would you likely receive an internal vision?

   _____

   _____

5. What are the four pointers in vision interpretation?

___

PRACTICAL PROJECT: EXTERNAL VISIONS

As you learn to hear from the Lord for yourself, you will come to realize how you receive revelation quicker on behalf of others! In this project I want to encourage you to use what the Lord has given you on behalf of others!

1. Come to the Lord and bring either your local congregation, family, or ministry associations before Him.

2. Pray as you are lead. If you feel a negative impression in your spirit, then do not progress, but if you feel a positive impression, go ahead (almost like an excitement - this is a sign you are praying in the right direction).

3. As you bring this group before the Lord note any pictures that come to your mind.

4. Then take those pictures and search the Word for explanations to the objects you see.

5. Use the following points to identify and interpret the visions the Lord has given you:

Picture:	Category:
	Discerning Spirit:
Characters:	**Objects:**
Interpretation:	

Picture:	Category:
	Discerning Spirit:
Characters:	**Objects:**
Interpretation:	

Picture:	**Category:**
	Discerning Spirit:
Characters:	**Objects:**
Interpretation:	

Picture:	**Category:**
	Discerning Spirit:
Characters:	**Objects:**
Interpretation:	

Page | 248 Lesson 21

EXERCISE: VISION EXAMPLE

Below is an example of a vision and its interpretation. Identify the specifics, then write your interpretation of the vision. Remember to dig into the Word for your answers! View my interpretation afterwards.

> **TWO BELLY BUTTONS**
>
> The other night while I was praying in the Spirit (tongues), I had a vision of a pregnant woman (7 to 9 months) who had 2 belly buttons! I was not praying with regards to anything specific – just general prayer.
>
>

a. **Vision category:**

_____

b. **Discerning spirit - positive/negative:**

_____

c. **Characters:**

_____

_____

_____

d. **Types and objects:**

_____

Colette Toach

e. Interpretation:

EXTRA NOTES

Lesson 22 - Four Pointers for Interpretation

Based on: *The Way of Dreams and Visions*, Chapter 22

As people start coming to you for ministry and interpretations, I know that you will begin to feel some pressure on you to give people answers. You may feel an obligation to perform. Never forget that it is the Holy Spirit who manifests the gifts to you, and He is the one who gives the revelation.

You can follow the steps and principles, but at the end of the day, if you do not get anything… you do not get anything! Perhaps you are not meant to get anything.

If you try to push beyond that, you will push beyond what God intends. You will end up doing more damage than good. Or you might end up saying something flowery, when the Lord wants you to be firm and bring a correction.

Don't find yourself getting caught up in that performance. It is a very real temptation. You get under the compulsion of always having to get revelation. You start to feel that receiving an interpretation is dependent on you entirely. No, that takes it out of the Lord's hand.

You only need to be a willing vessel. It is for the Lord to give the revelation.

There is no shame in saying, "I do not get anything right now."

I have given you a user's manual here and given you the steps to follow. However, if at the end of the day you do not get revelation, all of that flies out of the window. There is no instruction in the world that can make up for hearing the voice of God!

If you feel a block in your spirit perhaps the person is just not ready or the dream has no meaning. You will gain more respect by being honest than by trying to make something up and making a mistake.

People will not easily forgive you for sharing something that is wrong. However, they will be more than willing to listen again if this time you say, "God does not tell me anything. I will get back to you." By taking this stance, you will gain respect because the person will know that you are not there because of who you are.

You will be there because of who God is.

SHARE ONLY WHAT YOU RECEIVE

Do not add things to what you receive to try and "pad" your revelation. Share only what you see and what God tells you.

Share what you get and then stop. Do not push beyond that and add your own agenda. All of us have our little hobby horse or the latest thing we are reading.

Do not try to interpret those new revelations into everyone that comes your way! Do not try to bend what that person is sharing to come in line with what you are learning right now. No, keep it simple.

Share what God gives you. Share the vision you receive. Nothing more. Nothing less.

DON'T EXPECT EVERYONE TO LOVE IT

If you think that you will be the great interpreter and that everyone will be in awe of what God has given to you, I am going to burst your bubble.

If their dream indicates that their sin has given satan license, it is not often that someone will say full of joy, "Wow! Thank you for that. I see it all so clearly now. Satan has been given a foothold in my life through my own sin, and the solution is repentance before the Lord. I messed up and I need to look at my own beam. I will do that right now."

Not likely. Not everyone is going to love what you have to share, but this does not mean you should not share. No, share what you see and what God tells you whether it is what the person wants to hear or not.

What they do with what you share is up to them. The interpretation of Pharaoh's dreams were not very nice ones, but it was not for Joseph to force the king to action. He could only share the interpretation. It was for the king to make his mind up from there.

How about the interpretation to the baker? He gets told he is going to get strung up and have his flesh eaten by birds. Just great. And you thought you had to give some tough interpretations!

People will not always like it, but you must still speak the truth.

POINT TO A SOLUTION

Our solution is always Jesus Christ. At the end of the day, you are interpreting their dreams to bring them into a closer walk with the Lord.

The purpose is not to bring them into a closer walk with you. It is not to bring them into a greater understanding of what you have said or done.

Help and teach them to discern His voice, so that they know what He is saying. If you can do that, then you would have accomplished your job.

Do not finish an interpretation without pointing to a solution. If you have done that, even if you really messed up the interpretation, it does not matter. You have given them the one solution that counts more than any other.

If you can lead them to the source of all revelation, they can leave and figure it out for themselves in the future. The Lord can fix up your mess ups. He is good at that. In fact, He has been doing it now for a couple thousand years.

So be sure to follow the instructions and the steps I have given, but do not forget that it is the Lord who is in control. It is still the Holy Spirit who gives, takes away, and inspires. It is still the Lord that will give you the words to speak.

So let this be a rest. Let this be something that you enjoy. Before long, you will find people flocking around hearing what you have to say. Then because of their faith and hunger for God, you will get the revelations that they need.

This is an exciting journey and before you know it, your ministry car will be on the road again heading towards the next grand adventure that the Lord has in store for you.

QUESTIONS FOR REVIEW

1. **What would you do if you see a modern day object or symbol in vision that is not in the Word?**

   _____

   _____

   _____

   _____

   _____

2. **What do chains and a prison represent in vision?**

   _____

   _____

3. What does a heart represent in a vision?

_____

_____

4. How do you know when a vision is internal?

_____

_____

_____

_____

_____

PRACTICAL PROJECT: ULTIMATE GOAL

The ultimate goal that we are all headed towards is to become the image of Christ - to know Him and to walk with Him daily.

In this final project I encourage you to walk in a personal relationship with the Lord Jesus daily. You can keep doing this project for years to come and make it a part of your personal time daily as you spend time in His presence.

Try these 5 points every day for a week and you will notice a dramatic change in your personal spiritual life. Apply them for a lifetime, and you will bring change to the body of Christ!

1. **Journal every day - before you begin your day.**

    As you do this you will receive daily wisdom on how to face what lies ahead. By doing this you put on your armor and receive true wisdom. You cannot fail when you have received your direction from the Lord Himself for each day. You will always be in His will!

2. **Make note of all visions and dreams.**

   As you do this, you will begin to see a steady progress in your spiritual walk. You may forget a lot of the dreams and visions the Lord gives you, but as you look back on them in the months to come, it will encourage you to see how very far you have come!

3. **Spend time DAILY in the Word.**

   It is vital that you feed your inner man with the pictures of the Lord. Take a passage or chapter from the Word daily and meditate on it. Not just reading it, but using the principle I showed you of making the scriptures real, by converting them to mental images. These images will stay with you always.

4. **As often as you can – pour out to others.**

   This principle is most vital in keeping your spiritual life active! If you do not pour out, your inner stream becomes dead and stagnant. The anointing will decrease, and you will find yourself losing the sharpness on the spiritual gifts the Lord has given you. Pour out in encouragement, writing, speaking – anything that means tapping the anointing within you.

5. **Spend every spare moment speaking to the Lord.**

   You will become more familiar with the Lord as you integrate Him into every part of your day. Practice His presence often until He has become just like any other person speaking to you.

EXERCISE: IDENTIFY THE SYMBOLS!

Identify the possible meaning of these objects from the Word. Search in the Word for a positive and negative meaning of the object, then give a summary of how you would interpret this word. To identify the following objects, you would need to use a good concordance or look up each word in a bible software or CD that has good search capabilities.

Below is a list of objects and symbols:

1. Look each one of these up in your concordance. If you cannot find the exact object, look up an equivalent.
2. Note all your results.

A. ALTAR – See also: Sacrifice

Positive connotations/scriptures:
_____
_____
_____
_____
_____

Negative connotations/scriptures:
_____
_____
_____
_____

Your conclusion:
_____
_____
_____
_____
_____
_____

B. ARROW – See also: Armor

Positive connotations/scriptures:
_____
_____
_____
_____

Negative connotations/scriptures:
_____
_____
_____
_____

Your conclusion:
_____
_____
_____
_____
_____

C. AXE – See also: Sword

Positive connotations/scriptures:
_____
_____
_____
_____
_____

Negative connotations/scriptures:
_____
_____
_____
_____
_____

Your Conclusion:
_____
_____
_____
_____
_____
_____
_____

D. BABY – See also: Babe

Positive connotations/scriptures:

Negative connotations/scriptures:

Your Conclusion:

E. DARKNESS – See also: Light, Death

Positive connotations/scriptures:
_____
_____
_____
_____

Negative connotations/scriptures:
_____
_____
_____
_____

Your conclusion:
_____
_____
_____
_____
_____
_____

F. EAGLE - See also: Bird, Bat, Owl

Positive connotations/scriptures:
___

Negative connotations/scriptures:
___

Your conclusion:
___

YOUR FINAL GROUP PROJECT

With this being the concluding group project of this workshop, you could decide to have a small celebration and to discuss in a casual atmosphere what each one learned the most during this course.

Be open to take questions on anything else that they did not understand, and then end by ministering to each student.

1. Have a time of worship and prayer as a group.
2. Pray for each student one by one, speaking any revelation that God gives you.
3. Share any visions, minister inner healing, or speak any decrees over each student as God leads you.
4. If you do not get any revelation for a student, this is not a problem. Speak blessing on them and pray that the Lord will take everything they learned and apply it to their lives.

EXTRA NOTES

_____

_____

_____

_____

_____

_____

_____

_____

_____

Exercise Answers

Exercise Answers

Lesson 01

DREAM 1:

This is clearly a purging dream.

   a. Firstly, the events in the dream were directly related to current events.

   b. It was not a short quick dream, but one that went on and on throughout the night, with many scene changes.

   c. The emotions were high in this dream! The dreamer found themselves doing things and saying things that they would not normally do.

DREAM 2:

This is the healing dream.

   a. The dream involved a character from the past.

   b. Even though in reality the two parted on bad terms, in the dream they had reconciled.

   c. The person woke up refreshed and feeling positive.

So how did you do? If you did not get it right, do not be concerned, you will be getting a lot more practice as we move on to the next lessons.

Lesson 02

a. Firstly, this dream is internal because the dreamer is the star of the dream.

b. The character here would be the "friend" and the symbol the "achievers award."

c. If you read the dream through, you will notice the negative spirit on it. This award does not look like a positive thing. The characters involved do not have a positive impression either.

MY INTERPRETATION:

In this context the dream is internal and has a negative connotation. What I received from it is that you have 'worked' so hard that you have achieved the highest workers award! However, in our Christian walk we are redeemed by faith and without faith it is impossible to please the Lord. Although it would seem that you have been working very hard - in fact harder than anyone else, it is not what the Lord requires of you.

He does not require your works, but your faith, hope, and love. I encourage you to rest in the Lord and to stop all the striving. You will get His favor by simple childlike faith because our works are as dirty rags in His sight. Perhaps you have been experiencing a death or will be in the near future. Reliance on your abilities and strengths must die so that you can stand and say just like Paul: "Most gladly therefore will I glorify in my weakness, so that the power of Christ can rest upon me!"

It is not an easy road, but one you will pass through to promotion and victory!

LESSON 03

a. You can identify this as an internal prophetic dream firstly because the dreamer was the star of the dream and actively involved. Secondly some of the characters and symbols in the dream were familiar to him, while others were not. While his mentor was a common character, it is not every day that you find yourself on a mountain looking at baby eagles.

b. The character was obviously the mentor and the symbols were the eagles that were not quite mature yet.

c. The mentor would represent a father figure to this person, very likely the Lord in his dream. The eagles represent aspects of his ministry.

MY INTERPRETATION:

I am going to break this dream down bit by bit and show you how I interpret it ok? (The person's dream has two ** in front of it and my interpretation is in Italics).

** The dream began with myself and him looking in an eagles nest that was covered.

This dream is internally prophetic, relating to John's spiritual life. Reason: He is an active participant in the dream and there are symbols that are both common and uncommon to him here. I did a bit of searching on the word "eagle" in the Word and found these references to eagles in the Scriptures which I thought were relevant.

*"**Deuteronomy 32:11-12** - As an eagle stirs up its nest, hovers over its young, spreading out its wings, taking them up, carrying them on its wings, 12 So the Lord alone led him, and there was no foreign god with him."*

*"**Exodus 19:4** - You have seen what I did to the Egyptians, and how I bore you on eagles' wings and brought you to Myself."*

** As he uncovered the nest we saw that three eagles were inside.

I believe that that the nest and the covering speaks of the Lord (referring to the first scripture). The Lord has covered over and protected what is within John. I also believe that the 3 eagles speak of 3 specific ministries in this person's life. Perhaps 3 kinds of ministry function.

** The eagles were not immature, that is they were fully developed and had full plumage etc.

These gifts or ministries are not immature in this person. He has had them for some time, but they have simply been hidden. How long has John been saved? Has he had exposure to the Lord as he grew up? This dream indicates that the Lord planted something in his life some time ago already.

** My words were to not touch them and to not cover them back up again. End of dream.

You are his mentor, so I would say that you speak of the Lord in this dream. Are you perhaps a father figure to John? The Lord is saying that he is not quite ready to move into these ministries yet - he must wait until they are fully matured. Perhaps John feels that he is ready to "step out" but the Lord is saying that he must remain under covering for a while and mature fully first.

Stepping out means right now that he will fall flat. But as he continues to receive from you and grow under your mentorship, the time will come when you will release him to fly and then into the fullness of his ministry will come forward. For now however, he is still the disciple. I would encourage you to share my teaching with him entitled The Prophetic Child, I think he will be able to identify these signs in his upbringing.

Lesson 04

a. You can identify this as an external prophetic dream because the dreamer was not involved but rather an onlooker.

b. There are no characters in this dream, but many symbols. The earthquake and the house being the primary ones.

c. The earthquake refers to some kind of shaking. The house speaks of the Church.

MY INTERPRETATION:

Your dream is externally prophetic and speaks of the Church system - referring to the body of Christ universally. Your "mother's house" refers to the Church as we know it - the institutionalized Church. A mighty shaking in coming in the body of Christ.

The Lord has been speaking through His prophets for some time now with this warning. The old system is going to break apart and the new will be built. The Word says that there is no other foundation that is laid other than Jesus Christ, then in Psalm 127 David says that they who build a house without the Lord, labor in vain who built it. So know that the Lord is bringing an earthquake on the body of Christ, firstly to wake it out of its slumber and also to shake loose anything that is not of Him.

So was it the Lord who destroyed the house? No, the house simply fell apart because it was not built correctly. This is a warning dream of things to come, but it is also an encouragement that the Lord is about to move on His people as never before and bring fresh change that will correct the wrong building of the old foundation.

Lesson 08

a. This vision makes you feel good. You feel motivated and stirred within. It is definitely positive.

b. The characters and symbols are the Lord on a white horse, a sickle and the harvest.

c. Looking into the Word, the Lord on a white horse speaks of His majesty as in the book of revelation. The harvest and sickle speak of the work to come.

MY INTERPRETATION:

The Lord is well-pleased with you and has revealed Himself to you in a special way. Even though He is the King of Kings, He still comes down and gives you a hug. He is showing you that He is someone you can approach at any time and have a personal relationship with.

On the one hand He will protect you as your king and Savior, but on the other hand He wants to comfort and encourage you as friend and lover.

He has a work for you to do and He is not going to leave you to do this work by yourself! He is right in there doing the job with you. He does not expect you to take up the sickle and do all the work by yourself. No, the King comes from His horse and puts His hand to the sickle with you. Perhaps you have been feeling overwhelmed by the task ahead and do not feel that you are able to do it.

The Lord is saying that you do not need to do it by yourself! He will not only give you the tools you need, but will be with you every step of the way, showing you how! So be encouraged, the Lord is never going to leave or forsake you.

Lesson 15

VISION 1:

"The Candlestick" is a trance vision.

- ✓ Firstly, this prophet was in a sleep like state, because the angel had to "rouse" him.
- ✓ Another tell-tale sign is that all senses were involved in this vision. If you read further on in this passage you will see how he also hears the angels speak to him.

VISION 2:

"The Dove" is an open vision.

- ✓ Only John and Jesus saw this vision, no one else did.
- ✓ The vision was imprinted on their minds. They did not go into a trance but were very aware of their surroundings – all their senses were alive and they were in control of them.

VISION 3:

"The Glory of God" is an impression on the mind.

- ✓ This is the most common vision that we receive as believers.
- ✓ Steven saw this vision by himself.
- ✓ The passage says that he was full of the Holy Spirit, meaning that this was a revelation from the Lord for him. He saw into the spiritual realm with the eyes of the spirit – not with his natural eyes.

Lesson 20

a. Dream category: internal prophetic

b. Negative or positive: positive

c. Characters in the dream: person in dream, unidentified voice

d. Objects in the dream:

- Door: Speaks of new level of ministry.
- Key: Speaks of spiritual authority. In this case, it speaks of the apostolic ministry.
- Horizon: Speaks of what is to come. The circumstances and events surrounding this step.

e. Interpretation:

I believe this is a confirmation to line up with the other dreams the Lord has been giving you. It is time to step out now in apostolic training and application. You must now move to the practical part of apostolic training and begin using the key He has given you!

As you step out and use that key, your situation will fall into place. The Lord is waiting for you to make a move now. He has given you the preparation and He has given you the authority, now He waits for you to make the next move. As you make that move, He will then lead you to where you must go next.

I know it can be pretty scary - because you are stepping through that doorway alone! But as you do it the horizon WILL appear. We are here to encourage you but we cannot do this for you, this is a step you must make on your own.

Lesson 21

a. Vision category: internal vision (relates to person)

b. Discerning spirit: I discern a positive spirit

c. Characters: no characters

d. Types and objects: pregnant woman, two belly buttons

e. My Summary:

I did some digging in the Word for you. First I looked up the word "navel" in the concordance and then the word "womb."

This passage stood out to me when I looked up the word womb:

And the Lord said to her: "Two nations are in your womb, two peoples shall be separated from your body- one people shall be stronger than the other, and the older shall serve the younger." 24 So when her days were fulfilled for her to give birth, indeed there were twins in her womb. (Genesis 25:23-24)

and the passage I found for navel:

It will be health to your flesh, and strength to your bones. (Proverbs 3:8)

Navel here actually means umbilical cord.

The interpretation is this: you are pregnant with 2 visions. You have conceived twins and so there are two ministries or visions that are being birthed in you. These ministries will have their own lifeline (umbilical cord) and they will be separate - even though they come from you. They will each have their own function, and they will each carry out their own tasks. In fact, it is entirely possible that these two ministries may at first be seen to oppose one another in their difference!

I believe that the Lord has a call for you that goes beyond what you have comprehended up until now.

Colette Toach

LESSON 22

A. ALTAR

To pay the price for the call of God on your life.

Positive: To "burn your bridges"
Negative: Idolatry

CHARACTER SPECIFIC SYMBOL

POSITIVE

It could be that the Lord is asking you to give something up. The point of a sacrifice is to yield something up that is valuable to you. The most famous example of this in the Word is Abraham and Isaac.

If you feel that the Lord has been asking you to give something up and then you dream of an altar, it is a confirmation of what He is telling you. It is time to give that thing up to Him and let go.

> *Philippians 4:18 Indeed I have all and abound. I am full, having received from Epaphroditus the things sent from you, a sweet- smelling aroma, an acceptable* **sacrifice***, well pleasing to God.*

NEGATIVE

If you are having nightmares or negative dreams of ritual sacrifice, then there is an indication that something is wrong in your spiritual life.

Has there been a history of witchcraft or false religion in your family generations? If so, then the Lord is exposing a generational curse that needs to be dealt with.

If you wake from your dreams in fear, then this dream has no interpretation. It is a demonic attack.

UNIVERSAL SYMBOL

POSITIVE

Used as a prophetic symbol:

> Exodus 20:24 An **altar** of earth you shall make for Me, and you shall sacrifice on it your burnt offerings and your peace offerings, your sheep and your oxen. In every place where I record My name I will come to you, and I will bless you.

This speaks of death to the flesh. It speaks of giving up those things that hinder you in your work; of laying on the altar your sins and iniquity.

It also speaks of "burning your bridges," as Elisha did when he burned his cattle and the plow upon the altar.

I often see the altar of God when I enter the Throne Room in praise and worship. It is golden, and I imagine it is a duplicate of what Moses built in the ark of the covenant.

At one time I saw upon it a small lamb that had been slaughtered. The Lord placed the broken and bleeding lamb from that altar and placed it in my hands.

He said very clearly to me, "Take my blood and give it to my people. Go heal my people!"

At other times when I have seen an altar the Lord has said to me, "I need you to sacrifice those things that are important to you, so that I might take you to the next level." I have often been asked to "sacrifice my Isaac" on the altar of God.

NEGATIVE

May speak of idol worship and demonic rituals that were also prevalent in that time. To burn something on an altar that you should not be, speaks of "giving up" things that the Lord never asked of you in the first place. Determine if it is the Lord calling you to let something go, or if your flesh just wants to "be rid of something" and you are forcing His hand.

B. ARROW

Arrows speak of spiritual warfare as words are sent forth into the earth.

Positive: The word of God going forth
Negative: Negative words sent against you in the spirit

POSITIVE

Referring to deliverance and decree:

> *2 Kings 13:17 ... Then Elisha said, "Shoot"; and he shot. And he said, "The arrow of the Lord's deliverance and the arrow of deliverance from Syria;*

The arrow of the Lord speaks of deliverance and the Lord working on our behalf.

I have often seen a fiery arrow in the spirit, which indicates the word of the Lord going forth like lightening and accomplishing the work for which it was sent.

Seeing an arrow going out in the spirit also refers to speaking forth decrees like fire into the night sky.

Referring to children:

> *Psalms 127:4 Like **arrows** in the hand of a warrior, so are the children of one's youth.*

Arrows are also a picture of children, both natural and spiritual. Just like an arrow in the natural is prepared and then fired into a target, so also is it our job as parents to prepare and then send our children into the world.

When my parents were facing a divorce, the Lord showed my father how each of us were as arrows that were still newly cut from a green branch. The Lord said to him, that it was up to him to "keep the arrows straight" until the time came for us to be sent out.

NEGATIVE

The dark arrow in dreams and visions always speaks of the weapons of the enemy. They seek to destroy and cast down the righteous.

In the spirit I have often seen negative words and curses spoken over God's people as black arrows that pierce and cause theft, strife, destruction, and fear. To back up this revelation by the Word:

> *Proverbs 25:18 A man who bears false witness against his neighbor is like a club, a sword, and a sharp **arrow**.*

C. AXE

A weapon of spiritual warfare.

Positive: Completely destroying the work of the enemy
Negative: Refers to destruction or humiliation.

POSITIVE

> *Jeremiah 51:20 You are My battle-**ax** and weapons of war: for with you I will break the nation in pieces; with you I will destroy kingdoms;*

Seen in a positive light, we as the Church are an axe in the hand of the Lord. We are His weapon against the enemy. This represents strength and destruction against the works of satan.

It is a powerful, but crude, instrument and refers more to brute strength than precision. It not only tears down, but brings permanent damage. When a tree is cut off at the roots, it is completely destroyed! An axe is an aggressive weapon and denotes spiritual warfare that is going to be difficult and requires you to follow through for complete victory. A long journey is ahead of you – fight and do not give up!

NEGATIVE

> *Matthew 3:10 And even now the **ax** is laid to the root of the trees. Therefore, every tree which does not bear good fruit is cut down and thrown into the fire.*

The axe seen in a negative light speaks of separation and destruction. It separates the good fruit from the bad.

When I see an axe bringing a division in the Spirit, I know that the Lord is speaking of bringing a division between those who mean business with God, and those who do not.

In a situation where the axe is being brought to the root of a tree as in the Scripture above, I know that the Lord is speaking of removing an aspect from a person's life entirely. This can speak of bringing the flesh to death.

This vision taken literally, speaks of the Lord removing a ministry, position, or person that is standing in the way of His will. For God to accomplish this sort of division, he will use a prophet to send out a decree.

D. BABY

Babies have a twofold meaning. They represent being given a new ministry responsibility. Secondly they speak of having trust, vulnerability, and innocence.

In a negative light, they speak of immaturity.

CHARACTER SPECIFIC SYMBOL

POSITIVE

A baby speaks of a new life and a new aspect in your life and ministry. A baby boy often speaks of a teaching and leadership type of ministry, whereas a baby girl speaks of a more prophetic or creative emphasis in your ministry.

If you dream of a baby that suddenly matures beyond its age (for example it is a newborn that can walk already) this indicates that the new thing that has taken place in your life is going to mature fast.

If you dream of having twins, this speaks of having either a ministry or gaining a responsibility that is twofold or that has two different aspects to it.

The dream is indicating that you should nurture both aspects and not take one or the other.

If you dream that someone else you know hands you their baby, this could speak of that person giving you either their responsibility or ministry mandate.

This depends, of course, on what this person would represent in your dream. If they are an image to you of a ministry type, then it would speak of the Lord giving you this kind of ministry also.

If the person giving you the baby is a spiritual parent, then this would speak of them handing their mandate over to you.

If the person handing you the baby is someone that has a negative connotation in your life, then this would be negative and speak of you being put under pressure to take something you do not want or something that is not of the Lord.

NEGATIVE

If you dream that you lose your child or baby, it means that you have neglected and lost the promotion in the spiritual realm that God was giving you.

If you have been trusting God for something specific and dream that you lose a baby, it could mean that you have lost your faith or that a curse is causing that blessing to be lost.

If you dream of neglecting your baby, it means you have not been using your spiritual gifts.

If you dream that you are taking another person's baby, it means that you have taken on responsibilities that are not your own.

A baby and child also indicate that this spiritual gift is yet young in you. It means that you are yet immature in that calling.

UNIVERSAL SYMBOL

POSITIVE

Babies speak of a new life and also of trust. They speak of innocence and purity. They are not yet corrupted and have strong faith. This is why Jesus told us to be like little children. Children also speak of the blessing of the Lord.

If you see someone in the spirit with many children around them, it could be that the Lord is calling them to become spiritual parents. It can also indicate that the Lord has many blessings in store for them.

> *1 Peter 2:2 as newborn **babes**, desire the pure milk of the word, that you may grow thereby,*

Babies receive with innocence what they are fed and hunger for it. To see someone as a baby would indicate that the Lord wants them to receive without asking questions. To trust the Lord completely as Jesus explains in this passage:

> *Matthew 11:25 At that time Jesus answered and said, "I thank You, Father, Lord of heaven and earth, that You have hidden these things from the wise and prudent and have revealed them to **babes**.*

If you see someone you are ministering to as a baby in the arms of the Lord, the message is that the Lord wants them to rest in Him, to be a baby and to trust that He will care for them.

NEGATIVE

If you see a baby in the spirit, it could mean that the person you are ministering to is still a baby in their spiritual walk. If I am counseling a person and see them as a baby, this could also indicate hurts from the past that started at that age that need inner healing.

If you have a vision that is negative then it could also speak of birthing things that were not conceived by the Lord, but rather by the flesh or from the enemy.

Inner healing: If you are prophetic and you are ministering inner healing and see a baby that is hurt or upset, the Lord is showing you where the hurts for this person began. Ask them if anything traumatic happened at the age you see the baby as in your vision.

Actual events: In some instances, if you see a baby, the Lord could be showing you a real baby that this person had. Always share your vision with the person you are ministering to and ask them to clarify. Especially when you feel that the baby you are seeing in the spirit is not symbolic, but a revelation of actual events.

It could well be that the person is struggling over guilt from an abortion or was adopted as a baby.

E. DARKNESS

Opposite to everything light. This a picture of sin, deception, confusion and all the works of the enemy.

To walk in darkness means to be led astray or to be confused. As believers we are called to walk in the light.

Positive: A season of rest
Negative:

- Confusion
- The enemy at work

UNIVERSAL SYMBOL

POSITIVE

Sometimes the Lord makes things dark so that the enemy cannot see what is going on! He sent darkness as a plague on the Egyptians! Although we do prefer to walk in the light, sometimes the darkness forces us to rest and to wait on God instead of pushing forward with our own good ideas! A season of darkness has a simple message, "Be still and know that I am God!"

NEGATIVE

For the most part though, darkness does not have a positive picture as it is the opposite of light - which is the very essence of God! The Scriptures tell us that satan and his fallen angels (demons) dwell in darkness. So as light is the epitome of the Lord and His blessing, darkness is the epitome of the enemy and his curses! Jude says it very clearly here:

> *Jude 1:6 And the angels who did not keep their proper domain, but left their own abode, He has reserved in everlasting chains under **darkness** for the judgment of the great day.*

Light vs. Dark: Light, life, and love are used interchangeably in Scripture to often mean the same thing.

Darkness, hate (bitterness) and death are the opposite of these spiritual forces. Darkness also speaks of walking in confusion and being blind. It speaks of being in deception as in this passage:

> *1 John 2:11 But he who hates his brother is in **darkness** and walks in **darkness**, and does not know where he is going, because the **darkness** has blinded his eyes.*

F. EAGLE

A picture of the Holy Spirit and His ability to protect us and do warfare on our behalf.

Positive: Powerful work of the Holy Spirit
Negative: Destructive work of the enemy

CHARACTER SPECIFIC AND UNIVERSAL SYMBOLS

POSITIVE

There are so many positive connotations for the eagle, that you might have many of your own in addition to this book.

My favorite is a personal revelation the Holy Spirit gave me concerning hiding in the shadow of His wings.

I saw myself standing alone, facing the many attacks and pressures that I am used to facing daily. Then I saw a huge eagle come and stand behind me and extend its wings. As it stood behind me, I was covered by its shadow.

When I stood alone, I looked very small when others looked at me. But when that eagle was behind me, the size of His very shadow made them stop dead in their tracks!

Alone, I was helpless, but as I stood in His shadow, they saw His magnificence, and so I was protected!

*Psalms 63:7 Because You have been my help, therefore in the **shadow of Your wings** I will rejoice.*

Here is another passage that describes the Lord as an eagle:

*Deuteronomy 32:11 As an **eagle** stirs up its nest, hovers over its young, spreading out its wings, taking them up, carrying them on its wings:*

NEGATIVE

In a negative light, an eagle can also speak of destruction. The eagle is a bird of prey, and it tears that prey apart with its powerful beak and claws.

Here is a passage that indicates that an eagle in a vision or external dream, can indicate destruction and an attack from the enemy:

Habakkuk 1:8 ... their cavalry comes from afar; they fly as the eagle that hastens to eat.

WHERE TO FROM HERE

You do not realize how much you have grown in the last weeks! Not only have you learned to flow in dreams and visions, but you are now in a dialog with the lover of your soul – the Lord Jesus Christ!

Many things are about to happen. You are about to sense more in your spirit than ever before. In fact, these teachings just uncorked more than you could have imagined. This is the main reason why I use the Way of Dreams and Visions as the first course in our Prophetic School.

Now not everyone who flows in visions is a prophet, but if you feel that stirring within that says, "There is more!" Then your next step is to begin looking at some prophetic ministry workshops.

I suggest getting your hands on *Practical Prophetic Ministry* or enrolling in one of our schools (you can find the information at the end of this workshop)

WELCOME TEACHER!

Now it will surprise you to know that the best dream interpreters are teachers! Because of their hunger for the Word, they know how to break it down better than anyone!

So although you enjoyed this course, you might feel that you are not called as a prophet. No problem! It is quite likely that the Lord is leading you to be a pastor or to teach! Exciting times are ahead!

Why not take things up a notch? For you, I suggest the **How to Hear the Voice of God** workshop. Go through it yourself and then start a group and teach it to others. I have laid it out just for you! With a workbook to follow and a bonus DVD, you can start taking your church to a whole new level in the Lord.

You have the tools in your hands, all that is left now is for you to do it!

NEED SOMETHING A BIT "HEAVIER"?

You enjoyed this workshop, but you are hungry for more! You are familiar with spiritual warfare and are ready to dig deeper. Well then the perfect workshop for you next will be the **Spiritual Discernment Workshop**! With the same layout, this workshop has meatier teachings and projects that will challenge you!

Be warned though! It is not child's play! As the name suggests, it will take you into the realm of discernment and spiritual warfare. Get armed, but first... get trained. Pick up the *Spiritual Discernment Workshop.*

FOR THE APOSTLES

If you enjoyed hosting this group project, but want to start establishing more groups and studies, then I have the perfect tool for you. You need to set up your team! Get your hands on the **Everything is Awesome When you are a Part of the Team** book.

With group projects geared specifically towards team building, you can set up a structure in your church that will enable you to keep maturing and equipping the saints. Go to the next level! It is good to learn to teach and train, but for growth, teach others to train! There will be no limit to how far you will reach with the message God has given to you!

About the Author

Born in Bulawayo, Zimbabwe and raised in South Africa, Colette had a zeal to serve the Lord from a young age. Coming from a long line of Christian leaders and having grown up as a pastor's kid, she is no stranger to the realities of ministry. Despite having to endure many hardships such as her parents' divorce, rejection, and poverty, she continues to follow after the Lord passionately. Overcoming these obstacles early in her life has built a foundation of compassion and desire to help others gain victory in their lives.

Since then, the Lord has led Colette, with her husband Craig Toach, to establish *Apostolic Movement International,* a ministry to train and minister to Christian leaders all over the world, where they share all the wisdom that the Lord has given them through each and every time they chose to walk through the refining fire in their personal lives, as well as in ministry.

In addition, Colette is a fantastic cook, an amazing mom to not only her 4 natural children, but to her numerous spiritual children all over the world. Colette is also a renowned author, mentor, trainer and a woman that has great taste in shoes! The scripture to "be all things to all men" definitely applies here, and the Lord keeps adding to that list of things each and every day.

How does she do it all? Experience through every book and teaching the life of an apostle firsthand, and get the insight into how the call of God can make every aspect of your life an incredible adventure.

Read more at www.colette-toach.com

Connect with Colette Toach on Facebook! www.facebook.com/ColetteToach

Check Colette out on Amazon.com at: www.amazon.com/author/colettetoach

CONTACT INFORMATION

To check out our wide selection of materials, go to:

www.ami-bookshop.com

Do you have any questions about any products?

Contact us at: +1 (760) 466 -7679
(9am to 5pm California Time, Weekdays Only)

E-mail Address: admin@ami-bookshop.com

Postal Address:

    A.M.I.
    5663 Balboa Ave #416
    San Diego, CA 92111, USA

Facebook Page: http://www.facebook.com/ApostolicMovementInternational

YouTube Page: https://www.youtube.com/c/ApostolicMovementInternational

Twitter Page: https://twitter.com/apmoveint

Amazon.com Page: www.amazon.com/author/colettetoach

AMI Bookshop – It's not Just Knowledge, It's **Living Knowledge**

Copyright © Apostolic Movement International, LLC

www.ingramcontent.com/pod-product-compliance
Lightning Source LLC
Chambersburg PA
CBHW080424230426
43662CB00015B/2209